What Do I Do When . . . ?

How to Achieve Discipline with Dignity in the Classroom

Allen N. Mendler, Ph.D.

NATIONAL EDUCATIONAL SERVICE

Bloomington, Indiana   1992

Cover design by Joe La Mantia

Printed in the United States of America

Printed on recycled paper

ISBN 1-879639-21-1

Contents

Acknowledgments v

Introduction vii

1. What Motivates Misbehavior 1

2. Principles of Effective Discipline 31

3. The Process of Change 57

4. Effective Classroom Methods of Discipline 63

5. Dealing with Power Struggles 93

6. Unconventional Methods of Discipline 115

7. Working with Parents 151

8. Schoolwide Discipline 161

9. Concluding Thoughts 181

Bibliography 185

Acknowledgments

THIS BOOK IS AN EXTENSION of my work in *Discipline with Dignity* (1988), which I co-authored with Dr. Richard Curwin. Rick Curwin is a brilliant, creative educator with whom I have had the good fortune of sharing much of my professional life's work. Rick has made a profound contribution in the field of education through his humanism, caring, and concern for children.

I wish to thank the teachers, administrators, and other professionals who have attended workshops and seminars across the country for many years. Your enthusiastic response inspires me to continue my efforts at creating, expanding, and developing. The issues you address remain without absolute answers. It is the desire to help each individual child and teacher establish meaningful contact that motivates the continuation of my work in this field. I hope that this book provides more ways in which to work with students so that each may pursue his own dreams and hopes.

Nancy Shin did an extraordinary job in the editing of this manuscript. Her effort, support, and affection are very greatly appreciated. My gratitude to Alan Blankstein and the whole crew at NES for their outstanding work. In addition to the many whom I have thanked in previous works, special thanks are owing to Pat Dignan, Mary Ann Evans Patrick, Wanda Lincoln, Frank Koontz, Susan Sien, Sylvia Sklar, Georgia Archibald, Margo VanHanaghan, Susan LaRock, Barbara Mitrano, and Sue and Bruce Smith for their support. A very special thanks to Phil Harris at Phi Delta Kappa for his consummate warmth, caring, and professionalism. I also thank Gordon Dorway, Chris Boehm, and Jonathan Savage for their permission to cite them.

There are several poems sprinkled throughout the text. These were written by juvenile delinquent teenagers incarcerated at the Oatka Residential Center at Industry, New York. The emotion captured in their poetry was for me stirring and breathtaking. To protect their confidentiality, only their initials are signed. My thanks to them and to the facility director and friend, Moe Bickweat, for allowing me to look inside their hearts and share their thoughts with my colleagues. Oatka Center is the most child-centered, caring facility I have ever seen.

Finally, the writing of this book was done during a period of time in which Lisa, my daughter, turned two years of age and my sons Jason and Brian entered mid-adolescence. Their sacrifice of time, patience, and understanding will forever be appreciated. My wife Barbara has always been by my side, encouraging me to do what needs to be done. Her love and support have made it possible for me to complete this project.

Introduction

IN THE BOOK *Discipline with Dignity,* Rick Curwin and I sought to provide educators with the information needed to deal both effectively and humanely with children. Our focus was to show how the enhancement and preservation of a child's dignity is always essential. We highlighted the differences between consequences and punishments, showed the relationships among stress, motivation, teaching methods, and discipline problems, offered alternatives to lose-lose power struggles, and attempted to address ways of effectively engaging the difficult-to-reach learner who acts out frequently. The response to our work has been extremely gratifying and has given us many opportunities to help educators and schools create and implement *Discipline with Dignity* programs throughout the nation.

This book reviews and updates the principles upon which *Discipline with Dignity* is founded. It summarizes the key methods and describes some new approaches to difficult behavior. It answers many "What do I do when. . . ?" type questions about how the program can be applied in different situations.

When I was in third grade, my teacher took exception to something I had done. All I can really remember is this big person coming at me angrily, pinching me up by my cheek and scolding me while hauling me to the front of the room. I can still feel the humiliation, embarrassment, and hatred to this day. Mrs. McLean robbed me of my dignity that day, and I still haven't forgiven her. There is little else I remember about grade school other than how my teachers treated me.

Schools and teachers still largely rely on some variation of Mrs. McLean's punitive obedience model of discipline, which says, "Do it my way or else!" Behavior modification techniques are essentially sophisticated ways of manipulating others to do as we wish. The authority either rewards or punishes the behavior he wants to "shape." Unfortunately, in all such programs, children are unlikely to internalize the values that underlie the desired behaviors. In the best-case scenario, students act appropriately in the presence of the rewarder/punisher. They become dependent upon others to tell them what to do and how well they did it. Rarely do these programs teach children to become responsible for what they do and for what kind of people they are.

Most children who grow up to become teachers were not discipline problems in school. Most were taught to "respect" authority whether right or wrong. Since teachers were to be "respected," they were imbued with power, and even those who were mean and uncaring were listened to for fear of retribution or punishment. Those who did not obey were often publicly scorned and held up for daily ridicule. I will never forget "Stackler," a skinny, forgetful, disorganized classmate in fourth grade who seemed to be the object of daily verbal abuse by the teacher. As I watched him endure his daily torture, I remember learning to keep my mouth shut, pay attention, and take absolutely no risks in that class. Since many of us grew up obeying, we tend to expect the same from kids nowadays. When they do not do as we want, we tend to feel helpless, and then we become more punitive, figuring that we have to get "tough" with the kids in order for them to obey. Many of us become a current version of Mrs. McLean. The tougher we get, the more resistant our "at-risk" kids become. Exasperated, we seek help from parents or administrators. When they do not cure the kid of his disobedience, we get mad at them. After about 10 years, many of us have trouble getting out of bed in the morning with any energy to keep going. Some turn the anger against themselves and become depressed, while others become cynical, critical, and dehumanizing for self-protection.

What we must realize is that, while obedience models of discipline always had a down side, in today's world they simply no longer work. The only kids who behave as a result of "obedience" methods are those who have "respect" or fear authority. And most of them will eventually stop obeying unless they feel respected by those in authority. Kids who lack respect for authority find no reason to behave just because the teacher says that they should.

The problem is that many of us do not know specific ways to replace our obedience methods. The frustration is shared by John Mackovic, currently football coach at the University of Illinois, who has said that, years ago, a coach could invariably seek compliance by eyeballing a player and exclaiming:

"Go over and stand in the corner!"

But, with increasing numbers of kids not automatically "respecting" or "fearing" the coach, Mackovic proceeds to offer alternates, none of which is particularly effective:

"Please stand in the corner."

"How about if you went over and stood in the corner."

"How about us talking about you standing in the corner."

"Why don't I go over and stand in the corner for you!"

We must realize that, in our culture, most of us no longer respect others just because of their title or role. It is rare to find citizens who unfailingly "respect" their politicians. Even religious leaders are suspect following recent scandals. Nowadays, to be successful in a position of authority requires an ability to connect in a caring way by inspiring hope within others and by leading one's own life in a manner that models the message. We live in turbulent times in which there are few norms. The existence of a multicultural milieu, with children being raised in every imaginable family structure, requires that the contemporary teacher have an almost incomprehensible mix of firmness, love, patience, understanding, and flexibility. Never has it been more urgent that we understand the basic needs that motivate children's behavior so that our styles and strategies may adequately address the diversity that is today's norm.

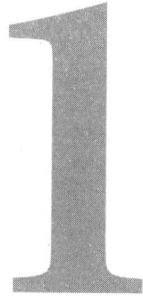

What Motivates Misbehavior

"**S**AMMY TALKS INCESSANTLY—nonstop! By the 50th reminder, I'm ready to stick a sock down his throat!"

"Out of 30 kids in my class, at least 10 are not following directions or are refusing to do things at any given time. As soon as I go to one corner of the room, a brushfire starts in another."

"Tim is an eight-year-old who has tons of potential and shows bursts of insight. However, most of the time, he either uses abusive language, falls out of chairs, crawls around, leaves the room, won't leave when asked, wrecks the restroom, or throws wet toilet paper."

"Leandra has a short fuse. She becomes physically abusive very quickly and has bitten people, thrown objects, hit, scratched, and pushed people."

"Joy complains about unfair treatment, makes noises, is unable to sit still, destroys property, steals, lies, and denies."

Students have changed. Experiences such as these have become all too commonplace in our schools. Many teachers become exasperated with politically motivated exhortations for more academic excellence while increasingly feeling burdened with kids flipping out. They are disgusted with comparisons to Japanese and Korean schools, which seem always to conclude that kids are doing better there than they are here. Often feeling pressured to cover the material so that scores will rise, many teachers are eager for *the* technique to use so that disruption to learning will end. There is no such technique! And this is neither Japan nor Korea. Children with behavior problems act out to satisfy their basic human needs, which too often are neglected by fragmented communities and unstable families. Solving discipline problems means doing things with kids that satisfy these basic needs. It means that teachers have no choice but to accommodate the diversity of today's youth. The alternative is business as usual, look for the quick fix, and burn out after a few years on the job. All kids need:

1. To feel and believe they are capable and successful

2. To know they are cared about by others

3. To realize that they are able to influence people and events

4. To remember others and practice helping them through their own generosity

5. Fun and stimulation

When any of these basic needs is unfulfilled, the child will seek other means of gratification. Some will turn to extended family members. Others will turn to friends, while some look to the streets. Gangs can be a powerful influence. So can teachers and schools.

I recently visited an urban middle school, where I followed the same group of "at-risk" kids throughout the day. These were a group of approximately 20 seventh- and eighth-graders at least two years behind in grade placement. In most classes, they were listless, inattentive, off-task, and disruptive. It was common for them to arrive without books and pencils while lumbering into room after room with an attitude reflecting anything but the desire for academic excellence. Equally common were the unstimulating, worksheet-dependent type of teachers with whom they came into contact. The lecture format was predominant, with at least half of each lesson focused on the teacher lecturing about responsibility. With few exceptions, kids were expected to work alone at their desks.

By fifth period, I had trouble keeping awake myself. I thought, "Is it any wonder that so many kids don't do homework or other work when we overload them with worksheet after worksheet in class?" What was really amazing was that so many kids continued to behave and try despite our best efforts at putting them to sleep.

Sixth period came, and I met Mr. Attwood. Attwood is a small, even frail-looking man who stood near the door with a friendly yet firm demeanor about him. As each student arrived, he made some kind of personal contact. A word to Larry, a glance to Jamil, a pat on Denise's shoulder were but a few of his warm ways of welcome. As metal-studded, leather-jacketed Felipe strolled in, Attwood tossed him a pencil. Sandra was one who arrived paperless, and Attwood took care of that by giving her some paper. The lesson began with a smoking test tube in front of the class. Attwood began to question his charges about their observations. Focusing on temperature, he asked if anyone would like to feel the tube. A girl toward the back said she would.

As the teacher gave the girl in the back the test tube, Cassandra blurted out from the other side of the room, "Can I go to Mr. P.'s office?" Attwood walked toward Cassandra as he continued to talk about the test tube. When he was about five feet away, he reminded her that he needed to see ten minutes of solid cooperation during the class. Following that, he would seriously consider her request. He walked back toward the girl with the test tube and asked her for her estimate of its temperature. Her response was, "Six degrees." "Interesting guess," Attwood said with wonder, enthusiasm, warmth, and affirmation, "and I can see how you thought that. You saw the smoke rising, just as it seems to do in ice and snow, and you probably figured that it is cold. But at six degrees a person would hardly be able to hold it because it is so cold. You probably meant 60 degrees." The girl's look said, "Oh, yeah!" A few minutes later, Attwood interrupted himself in mid-thought, went back toward Cassandra, and said, "Thanks for the cooperation. If you still need to leave, now would be a good time." Cassandra did not budge. As engrossed as the others, she said, "Nah, I can go next period."

Throughout the class, Mr. Attwood did so many little but meaningful things to address the *basic needs* of each of these students. It was no accident that virtually every student in that class was motivated, achievement-oriented, and well behaved. Attwood realized that hope needs to precede responsibility. He instinctively knew that when students chronically come unprepared and turned off, they first need to believe in their ability to be successful before they learn to be responsible. These were not the same kids that I had seen during the first five periods, and this was certainly not the same teacher.

BASIC NEEDS THAT MOTIVATE BEHAVIOR

CAPABLE / SUCCESSFUL

My life is sad but beautiful

Loving but filled with hatred.

I'm looked upon as the underdog,

But I know I'm somebody

And more than that I'm myself

My mind is free

But my body is shackled.

The door of hope is locked,

The key to life is in my mind.

—S.H.

All kids need to know that their lives have value and they can be successful. They need to believe that their efforts can make a real difference in their lives. Mr. Attwood gave youngsters hope by affirming each answer they gave before he sought to correct. He took a lot of the responsibility for their not getting the right answer by saying such things as, "I must not have made that very clear," and, "I can see what you must have been thinking," preliminary to correcting their answers. He read sample answers from a homework or classroom assignment and expressed genuine praise while noting how it could be even better if . . . . The kids then knew that they could "correct" the work for an even better grade.

Kids who are discipline problems often have a history of failure. There is a powerful relationship between poor academic performance and poor behavior. It is painful for people to be told repeatedly that they do not measure up. Such mental abuse causes damage to self-esteem, and many kids eventually withdraw or act out in protest. It is not surprising that most kids choose to be bad over being stupid if they view these as their only viable options. These students need to know that they can legitimately succeed and that their successes will be recognized. With some students who have become very turned off, disbelieving, and hopeless, it is sometimes necessary to make it impossible for them to "fail" in order for them to believe that success is possible.

I am reminded of Joey, a turned-off, disruptive eleventh-grader who had failed everything. The last quarter had just begun when I met with him to assess how he and school could become a better match. As Joey asserted that nothing was wrong and he needed no guidance, I reminded him that he had failed everything and offered the example of 12% on his report card for English. Joey became annoyed. "You really pi— me off," he responded. "I'm doing better in English and you're bugging me about this? Did my English teacher tell you that on the last test I got a 50 and on the paper due last week I got a 55? Can you count? I've improved 43 points." I practically fell off my chair. From Joey's perspective, he was improving, yet, as educators, rarely do we see a failing grade as representing any kind of improvement. Kids such as Joey need genuine acknowledgment that we see the progress represented by a "better failing grade" in order to maintain any hope. Otherwise, they quickly sink back to the level of a 12.

Hope in a school setting is best accomplished through helping kids confront real problems and find new cognitive, social, or emotional ways to solve their problems. Students develop increased feelings of competence and mastery, which provide the fuel for them to tackle the next uncertainty or challenge.

It is disturbing that so many self-esteem programs in schools are really little more than ineffective Band-Aids. Too often, self-esteem is reduced to Thursday afternoon between 1:00 and 1:30. An activity of the touchy-feely variety is introduced, and everybody is supposed to wind up feeling good and enriched. Self-esteem half-hour ends with everybody going back to business-as-usual. The blue jays, a.k.a. the bright kids, go off to silent reading; the redbirds, alias academic mediocrities, join together for reading group; while the robins, whom the world really knows as the "dummies," head off for remediation. If we really want to address self-esteem, the issue is giving kids the hope that their effort and initiative will result in mastery and success.

For many kids who range from mediocre to poor in their school performance, it takes a lot of courage for them to keep trying. Giving up or becoming disruptive are sensible alternatives (to them) when they are put into situations in which mediocrity is the best possible outcome. This writer learned long ago that his spatial skills are not among his chief talents. Receiving a poor score in "map reading" on the Iowa tests was an early objective measure of this weakness. Another was in seventh-grade "shop" class, when I had to plane a piece of wood as the first step toward making a basket. I could not get this piece of wood level. I recall my supportive teacher struggling to keep back the laughter as he looked at my now three-inch, off-center remnant, the only remaining logical use of which was kindling. The acquisition of every skill in that class felt like torture. I recall immense relief as the semester ended and I no longer had to face the vise, wood, level, and other tools. For me, trying harder did not provide much payoff and trying even harder would have meant taking time from other interests that I found more gratifying. To this day, I get anxious when I see or smell I.A. materials.

I recently set out to put up a swing set for my two-year-old daughter. As I took the pieces out of the carton and looked at the diagram of directions, I felt that I was again taking the "map-reading" Iowas. I may just as well have been looking at an aerial view of Tibet. I decided to save myself the anguish of trying harder and failing by hiring a handyman to set it up.

I believe that some of the automatic messages that we give to kids, such as, "Try harder," "Put in more time," "You can do it if you put forth your best effort," and "All I want is your best effort," are often ineffective and harmful. How long should any reasonable person put forth his best effort before concluding that it is better to put his best effort elsewhere? No child begins school not putting forth his best effort. Everyone wants to do well and be successful. However, when we incessantly evaluate performance and narrowly define the skills that comprise school intelligence, it is easy to understand that many students logically decide to put their efforts elsewhere.

My sons provide good examples of this process at school. One is extremely gifted academically, musically, and athletically. His biggest problem is deciding where to park his many gifts at any given time. My other son is a socially engaging boy with some, but not considerable, academic talents. He was highly motivated and largely successful through the early years. His teachers reported that he was in the highest skill groups for math, reading, and spelling because of his high motivation. By fourth grade, the picture was changing. He was no longer able to sustain success in the highest groups and was placed in the middle groups. His motivation began to wane. By fifth grade, he was less motivated to work hard in school and more motivated to have fun with his friends. By sixth grade, his fun with friends was at times becoming sufficiently disruptive to occasionally warrant a detention, much to the mortification of his father. After the second or third detention of that sixth-grade year, I recall, I became frustrated with him and I let him know. I had to fight the energy to either hit or verbally abuse him. I used a variety of I-messages to let him know how disappointed and frustrated I was. After what seemed like an eternity, Brian began to cry. Through his tears, he tried to express his own frustration. "Dad," he said finally, "I just can't do it. I can't be successful at school. Do you have any idea what it is like to try hard and still get a C? Having fun with my friends is far better. I hate school, and I wish I didn't even have to go!"

He then expressed what it is like growing up in an achievement-oriented family with a father who writes books, a mother who teaches, and a brother who is Number One at everything. His frustration was intense. I realized that I was contributing to it. As I listened to him, I recalled the many times I had tried to help him with homework but, after the third or fourth time that mastery of the concept remained elusive, the edge of annoyance and irritation showed in my voice. I have no doubt he detected this. My nonverbals were confirming his own worst fear—"I must be stupid."

From that point forward, Brian was able to begin defining for himself some school goals for which he could feel proud. There are still times when his discouragement becomes evident and he wants to quit. I have learned that it is far better to remind him that it requires courage and guts to continue when things are not going well. Kids need to hear that it is both normal and understandable to want to give up when the feedback is at best mediocre. The challenge is to access the courage that they need to continue in order to achieve perhaps a longer-term goal down the road. A child is helped when she hears, "Wow, I know reading is tough for you. I know you sometimes feel like giving up. You have a lot of guts to keep trying hard. I am proud of you!"

CARING / BELONGING

I never knew a night so black

Light failed to follow on its track,

I never knew a storm so gray

It failed to have its clearing day.

I never knew such bleak despair

That there was not a rift, somewhere.

I never knew an hour so drear,

Love could not fill it full of cheer.

—J.R.

The social factors that negatively affect a child's self-esteem, decision making, and behavior are well documented: alcoholic parents, peer pressures, the media, drug abuse, kids rearing each other, preoccupied parents, poverty, and homelessness. Approximately two million children are abused in our country each year. Recent data from forensic psychologist and attorney Charles Patrick Ewing predicts a coming "epidemic" of juvenile homicide. The number of youths arrested for murder nationwide more than doubled between 1984 and 1989 to more than 2,000. He predicts that by the year 2000 we could be looking at 6,000 or more juvenile homicides a year. Schools are already seeing increasing numbers of children at younger and younger ages coming to school with weapons, holding teachers and students hostage to their violent proclivities.

There are simply too many children who feel unloved, unimportant, and inferior. Depressed and unbonded, many project their hurt onto others through targeted or random violence. With easy access to deadly weapons, the chances of serious injury increase.

It is absolutely essential that the basic need that all people have to be cared for gets met. Every child needs to feel special and loved in order to become bonded. If she does not, then the need will not disappear—it will simply be met elsewhere—by the drug dealer, pimp, or gang. It is no accident that disenfranchised kids find each other and together feel a sense of power and control that each individually lacks.

The most basic expressions of caring are essential both to prevent discipline problems from occurring and to deal with them effectively when they do occur. I am reminded of Gaston Leroux's extraordinary story *The Phantom of the Opera,* about a hideously scarred, tortured, and lonely man who desperately seeks the caring and love of the beautiful Christine of the Paris Opera. Thwarted in his efforts to have the leaders of the opera do as he wishes, he threatens and then carries forth a series of evil deeds. All the while, he seeks her love but has to do battle with Raoul, the handsome rival, suitor, and actual lover, for her affections. As the final act unfolds, the Phantom has both Christine and Raoul captive in his dungeon. Christine has a choice: either remain with the Phantom and spare her lover or sacrifice her own life by choosing the man she does not prefer. While she clearly hates this "Catch-22," after a moment she says to the Phantom, "Pitiful creature of darkness, what kind of life have you known? God gave me courage to show you—you are not alone!" She emotionally wraps her arms around the Phantom's neck and kisses him passionately. Her choice is made: she will remain with the Phantom. Touched at his core of humanity, the Phantom gives in to what his heart knows is right. He releases Christine and Raoul. The chain of bondage is freed only after the Phantom unexpectedly receives the genuine affection and bonding he has been living without.

As I wrote in an article for *Family Life Educator,* it occurs to me that there are many "phantoms" in the classrooms of

America: deeply hurt children who lack a feeling of belonging and who are walking wounded, often masked. Some have hardened themselves to avoid the pain of more rejection. Many reject others to avoid being rejected first. Some suffer silently, like the proverbial kid who has it all on the outside but feels barren and vulnerable on the inside.

It is incumbent upon all of us to realize that each of us can be a critically important messenger of humanity by reaching out and giving a child the gift of our caring. A touch on the shoulder, greeting at the door, hug, smile, word of interest, or listening ear are a few of the ways to reach out and make emotional contact with kids who act out because they hurt. As Brendtro et al. suggest, many children who seek to belong can have "their unmet needs addressed by corrective relationships of trust and intimacy." We have noted that such teacher practices as sending home positive, caring, genuine notes to parents, calling a child at home to express concern or to share an appreciation, targeting one or two children a week who are in need and giving a few extra minutes of personal attention promote bonding and often pay dividends in the form of improved behavior. The growth and popularity of cooperative learning as an effective instructional modality attests to the hunger felt by many children for a sense of nourished belonging with others.

In the May 1991 issue of *The Monitor,* the American Psychological Association's newsletter, a debate about the relative benefits and disadvantages of black immersion schools was offered. James Jones said, "If you pay attention systematically to people, and show that you care about them, you very often will produce a positive kind of effect." Whether it be black immersion schools, native children on the reservation, or "mainstream" youth, we must get about the business of "systematic caring."

POWER / CONTROL

When my daughter was approximately one year old, I recall her sitting in her highchair with a peanut butter and jelly sandwich. She had recently been introduced to "people" food and was gobbling away. When she had eaten enough, she mushed the remaining sandwich in her hand and held it over the edge of her highchair, about to drop it. Before she did so, she made eye contact with me and said, "No, no, no," while she released the contents.

Children, like adults, need to feel that they can influence people and events around them. The need for power and control is central to human existence. Without breaking the rules of those in authority, children could never establish themselves as independent, functioning people. They would feel trapped, merely extensions of adults, and later need to break out of these chains. Children who are deprived of opportunities to safely break rules may come to feel powerless and out of control.

A central theme of "Discipline with Dignity" is helping kids who view themselves as victims develop an "internal locus of control." Students who are "discipline problems" generally view others as responsible for the bad things that happen to them. "I did it because . . . she stared at me, called my mama a name, pushed me, etc." Rarely do such students see how they influence what happens to them. Our observations tell us that the vast majority of disruptive students actually feel quite powerless. They "press others' buttons" as a way to feel in control.

The most effective way of helping kids learn that they can control their destiny in school is to provide opportunities for them to be decision makers. Students can become key decision makers by developing classroom rules and consequences through a process called the "social contract." In such circumstances, peers are much more likely to provide reminders when fellow students break rules, than they are in conventional class-rooms where teachers have to enforce all of the consequences because the system is "owned" only by the teacher. Teachers who have created social contracts with their students have reported that virtually all of the rules developed by the students are the same as those the teacher would have made by herself. But compliance is much higher because students have ownership in the classroom system. (See pp. 49–62 for details.)

In addition to the social contract, helping students develop an internal locus of control can best be accomplished through (1) increasing student awareness, (2) providing choices, (3) predicting, and (4) planning.

1. *Increasing student awareness.* Ask the question, "What?" not "Why?" If you ask a student why she did or did not do something, you encourage explanation or excuse-making. It is natural for people to look outside of themselves for the answer when asked a why question. "Why are you hitting Sally?" will usually be answered with a "because she" answer. When the goal is to get behavior to stop *and* to encourage learning responsibility, focus the child's attention upon her own behavior. Asking "what" questions does that. Instead of asking, "Why are you slapping Billy's head?" ask, "What are you doing?" If the child says, "Nothing," or starts blaming someone else, ask a follow-up question: "What are you supposed to be doing?" Reserve your "why" questions for when you and the child have lots of time to explore the issue.

2. *Providing choices.* In most schools, students are told for six hours every day where to go, what time to be there, how long to take for basic biological necessities, which learning is relevant, what to learn, and how their learning will be evaluated. Some students rebel as a way of

voicing their dissatisfaction with this lack of power. To truly empower students, we must give them real choices. How can someone become a good decision maker unless he is faced with the responsibility of having to make choices? The wise teacher provides opportunities wherever possible for students to practice this skill. There can be choices every day. Students can be given ten math problems and told to choose any five that will best teach them how to multiply. Decide each day who will be line leader. When rules are broken, kids can have a real choice: "What will best help you to stop—giving yourself a warning, writing a plan, or inviting Mom in for a problem-solving meeting?"

3. *Predicting*. Students who feel in control are better able to predict the consequences of their actions than those who do not. Often, their lives have been much more predictable. They can count on dinner at 6:00, a parent asking them about their day, being disciplined for staying out too late. By contrast, students who are poor at anticipating consequences have often had unpredictability as the hallmark of their lives. They need help in learning this important skill. A caring teacher who has an interesting, varied, and predictable routine provides an important structure for such students. Questions to ask that teach one to hone the skill of prediction: "What do you think will happen if . . . ?" "When can I count on your doing . . . ?" "If so-and-so did such-and-such, what are all the things that might happen?"

4. *Planning*. A feeling of being in control increases when one is armed with a plan of attack. Many students act out because they just do not know another way or they only know the one that gets them into trouble. A plan is a specific, detailed set of guidelines developed by the

student to be used the next time a set of similar circumstances occurs.

SITUATION

The situation that follows shows the process used by a teacher in working with a student to devise a plan. Notice how she is reflective, willing to listen, persistent yet respectful. She shows how to deal with resistance and to help the student overcome obstacles in the way of better behavior.

Teacher: Johnny, you seem to be angry with me lately.

Johnny: You bet. You don't treat me fair. If anything goes wrong, it's my fault.

Teacher: You feel that I don't treat you fairly, that I accuse you unjustly.

Johnny: Yeah! You always do it!

Teacher: I'm always blaming you for everything.

Johnny: Yeah! Jake was talking, but is he here? Oh, no. He's your favorite. He never gets into trouble. It's always me. Where's Jake?

Teacher: You feel I'm unfair that I always pick on you. You say Jake was talking and that he's not here. Johnny, I want you to know that I will not talk about one student to another. Is there anything else you'd like to tell me?

Johnny: Well, it's not fair! He was doing it, too!

Teacher: What were you doing?

Johnny: We were both talking. He told me . . .

Teacher: What were you supposed to be doing?

Johnny: Be silent until the directions were given. But he was talking, too.

Teacher: Johnny, you want to know why Jake isn't here. I will not gossip about another student. Now, you have said you were supposed to have been silent. Do you have a plan that you could use to remember this?

Johnny: No.

Teacher: Could you come up with a plan to remember to practice this rule?

Johnny: No.

Teacher: If you were to come up with a plan, what would it be?

Johnny: I don't know.

Teacher: We'll just sit here and let you ponder a plan.

(*Allow time to pass.*)

Johnny: I guess I could come up with a plan. Maybe I'll be the last one to come to the gym. That would help me be quiet.

Teacher: What if your friends were coming in with you and you just had to tell them something?

Johnny: I might talk.

Teacher: How would you avoid talking in the gym then?

Johnny: I couldn't.

Teacher: Would your plan work?

Johnny: No. Maybe I'd better be the last one to leave the classroom.

Teacher: Why would that work?

Johnny: Well, my friends would be ahead of me.

Teacher: What if your friends wanted to tell you something that was really interesting?

Johnny: I'd tell them to shut up.

Teacher: What would remind you to tell them to shut up?

Johnny: When I go through the fire doors. That'd be a reminder.

Teacher: So you say that you're going to use the fire doors as a reminder?

Johnny: Yep. When I go through the fire doors, that's a reminder for me to be quiet.

Teacher: All right. Let me see if I have this correct. You are going to use the fire doors as a signal for you to stop talking. What about being the last one in the gym?

Johnny: I'm going to do that too.

Teacher: All right, Johnny, it seems that you have a plan. Please write it down.

Johnny: I already said I was going to do it!

Teacher: Yes, Johnny, and I appreciate that. Now, I want to have you write it down.

Johnny: You don't trust me. I said I'd do it.

Teacher: You feel I don't trust you even though you told me you'd do it.

Johnny: Yeah!

Teacher: Johnny, I want you to write the plan down and give it to me so that we can avoid a situation like this in the future. Just in case this plan doesn't work, we need to know what part of it you need to re-work.

Johnny: All right, I will.

There are many group and individual strategies that enable children to increase their internal locus of control. With proper guidance, students are quite capable of solving problems among themselves. Inviting a student to solve a problem with the teacher can be quite empowering. "Bill, when you come late to class and the door shuts, it breaks my concentration and I have trouble teaching. Any suggestions on how we can solve this problem?" Sometimes, putting the whole group to work can make a big difference. "There's been way too much hurtful name-calling. In groups I want you to (1) discuss why people call each other bad names and (2) suggest what we can do in this class to make this problem stop."

Small things that adults think little about can make important contributions toward positive empowerment. Children gain a positive sense of power when we are polite to them. A student feels special when you ask for her opinion. Saying "please" and "thank you" models respect. Apologizing for intentional or unintentional hurts provides the right kind of attention. Be personal in giving feedback. I recently met with a boy who had gone out for the high school baseball team and not made it. Will was motivated for baseball. He was among a handful of players who came to optional "before-tryout" workouts that were held at 6:30 A.M. From his perspective, he had a good tryout and he thought that he had done plenty to make the team. When cuts were made, they were posted *in writing* outside the coach's office. When he saw his name, Will felt humiliated and devastated. Not once did the coach personalize the cut, and Will never felt comfortable approaching him for an explanation. For several weeks, Will was depressed, angry, and confused.

While there is no good way to be the bearer of bad news, as educators we must go out of our way to protect and enhance the self-esteem of the students entrusted to us. There is no doubt that a personal few moments of one-on-one contact, in which the coach gave genuine feedback (i.e., you need to work on your hitting ... I just didn't have room for another infielder ...) and then thanked the student for having put out the effort, would have enhanced rather than destroyed the dignity of this boy.

Facilitating positive empowerment means looking for opportunities for children to be in control of events around them.

GENEROSITY / HELPING

I regret the mistakes that I did make.

And also my feelings of no give and all take.

And for once in my life I'm ready to change.

But the solution to the problem is well out of range.

—D.L.

It is interesting to watch groups of toddlers and preschoolers interact with each other. There is invariably a child in distress who is either crying or having a tantrum. Just as regularly, there are other toddlers who approach their distressed peer cautiously, perhaps with "blanky" in hand. They no doubt sense that they need to be careful because this distressed toddler may bite, hit, push, etc. There are, after all, needs for "power" that all children have. This possibility does not, however, halt their forward march. They continue their cautious approach forward, and, as they arrive, a helping hand is often extended in the form of sharing a toy, touching the shoulder of the toddler, patting him, stroking his hair, even giving a hug. Quite often, others will come looking for the teacher/caregiver to voice the need for help. I have seen this type of interaction occur repeatedly among and between cross-cultural groups, and I have concluded that the need to reach out and give to others is as basic as the need to survive. In fact, when survival is at issue (during earthquakes, ice storms, tornadoes, floods), stories of people helping each other are commonplace.

Even newborns are thought to show behaviors associated with empathy toward others. In Simner (1971), studies are cited which showed that infants were more likely to cry when they heard another infant's crying than they were when they heard other noises of equal intensity. Zahn-Wexler and Radke-Yarrow (1982) found in a study of preschoolers that nearly 90% shared with, helped, or comforted another child at least once during a 40-minute observation of free play. Alfie Kohn (1990) has eloquently written about children's natural feelings of altruism and empathy. Luks (1988) described a "helper's high" that was linked to relief from stress-related disorders such as headaches and voice loss, even diseases such as lupus and multiple sclerosis.

Some children lose touch with their natural need to help when they shut down from the physical or emotional pain inflicted upon them. Reawakening this need can be healing and spiritually uplifting and can improve behavior. Teachers have frequently reported positive changes in students who are put in situations in which they are empowered to help others. The increase in self-help groups, wherein people who share common problems come together to help each other, is further testament to the power of helping.

In my book *Smiling at Yourself* (1990), a number of suggestions are offered for parents and teachers to engage the natural need in children to help. I describe a program in which juvenile-delinquent youth become clowns and then go out to nursing homes, hospitals, and preschools to brighten the day of others. The "hardened" boys in this program transform into caring, thoughtful "menschen." Within a regular school setting, tutoring and big-brother/sister programs, in which older kids help younger kids, can be beneficial to all.

As Brendtro et al. share in *Reclaiming Youth at Risk* (1990):

> [W]ithout opportunities to give to others, young people do not develop as caring persons. Some may be involved in pseudo-altruistic helping or they may be locked in servitude to someone who uses them. Others plunge into lifestyles of hedonism and narcissism. The antidote for this malaise is to experience the joys that accrue from helping others.

STIMULATION / FUN

A smile is cheer to you and me

The cost is nothing—it's given free.

It comforts the weary—gladdens the sad,

Consoles those in trouble—good or bad.

To rich and poor—beggars or thieves

It's free to all of any belief

A natural gesture of young and old,

Cheers on the faint—disarms the bold.

Unlike the blessings for which we pray,

It's one thing we keep when we

Give it away.

—J.R.

"That class is enjoyable . . . . Mr. Jones makes science interesting . . . . Mrs. Smith lets us ask questions and she really listens . . . . Mr. Vera is funny. He makes us laugh . . . . Miss DeLorm is neat. She tells us how it is for her."

These kinds of comments from kids illustrate that stimulation is an effective antidote for discipline problems. Children who get into trouble the most often at school attribute their problems to "boredom." While for some the leading issue may more realistically be poor school self-concept, it is imperative that as educators we make our classes as stimulating and enjoyable as possible. The value of what we have to offer depends largely on how we communicate, and good teaching requires elements of entertainment. Teachers who vary their style of presentation and who are sensitive to the different learning and intellectual styles of their students tend to have more motivated classes and fewer discipline problems.

Howard Gardner (1983) and Thomas Armstrong (1987) remind us that the focus of most school presentations tends to best suit those learners who are most competent with receiving and processing language and/or logic. We pay less attention to those who learn well interpersonally (with others), independently, musically, kinesthetically, or spatially. Providing adequate stimulation for learning requires that we present content in ways that accommodate these learners as well as the others.

School should be rich with moments of fun and laughter. In an era of media blitz, we must offer novelty in the presentation of content to spark interest in students. Further, to the extent that learning is made "personally relevant," kids are likely to see how the content can enrich their lives and their interest will be aroused. The question "Why do we have to know this?" needs an answer other than, "To get a good job someday . . . . Someday you'll understand . . . . Because it'll be on the test . . . . Because I told you so," if interest, motivation, and real learning are to occur. Comments and practices that devalue or dismiss student concerns often lead to anger or, even worse, apathy. That sets the stage for "unmotivated" problem behavior.

An energizing, enthusiastic approach to content is the surest way to make class motivating. At times, good wholesome laughter is a great way to defuse tension and build relationships. As you smile and joke casually with students, you demonstrate your concern for them as people. Luckner and Humphries (1990) point out that:

> *funny spontaneous things happen in every classroom, providing opportunities for shared laughter. A wise teacher will take time to enjoy those occasions with students, using them to improve classroom communication and to make the teaching/learning process more enjoyable for everyone involved.*

Gentile and McMillan (1978) wrote:

> *[F]or purposes of inner harmony and peace, no single human phenomenon is as healthy, spontaneous, honest and soothing as laughter. Unfortunately, opportunities for classroom humor may be overlooked by educators, who see it as an inappropriate distraction from the standard curriculum.*

Laughing probably helps people live longer, and, even if it doesn't, it certainly contributes to people living more happily. William Fry (1989) noted five seconds of belly laughter provides the cardiovascular equivalent of 10 minutes of strenuous rowing! Studies and interviews with students consistently rate "sense of humor" as being a very highly regarded characteristic in teachers.

There are many times in which a light moment and dignified humor can defuse potentially explosive classroom situations. Inappropriate student behavior in a group provides for such opportunities; it is at these moments that power struggles usually escalate. Disciplinary moments provide high drama in the classroom. There is a room filled with 20 or 30 people as one or more make a bid for control. This is much more interesting to most than working on times tables. Feeling challenged, the teacher looks at a classroom full of inquisitive faces who are often nonverbally (if the teacher is lucky) but clearly saying to her, "What are you going to do about it?" The teacher is concerned with losing the respect of the class, and the tendency is to get tough. This usually leads to a confrontation and perhaps a toss out of class to the principal's office. As the student leaves, ears get flicked, a chair is tipped, and kids are "accidentally" bumped before he finally reaches the door.

Just before parting, the student may offer an editorial comment about the class such as, "This f——in' class s——s." Fifteen minutes later, back comes the kid, often with a smirk on his face, a strut in his walk, and a "can't-do-nothin'-to-me" attitude. Even the best principals in the world are limited by their ability to influence many of the inappropriate behaviors offered by students.

While there are certainly times that disruption warrants a student needing to leave the classroom, I have found that humor can "work" at least as well if not better at defusing many of these moments before they get out of control. Just imagine how the student and class would react if you responded to the inappropriate behavior by saying something like, "I think I just heard Billy use some bathroom language, and I'll bet most of you heard it too, because as I look out at you, you look as if you're wondering what I'm going to do about this. How many of you are actually wondering what I'm going to do about this? Well, let me tell you that I just have no idea whatsoever right now what I'm going to do about this because I need to think this over. Billy looks upset now, and as soon as he and I have some time to figure out what's going on, we'll need to find a solution. But right now today's lesson is about . . . "

Finally, there may be times when you can become a bit more bizarre by saying, "I don't know what I'm going to do about this, but I sure know what I'd like to do about it. How many of you would like to know what I'd like to do about it?" At this point, you can expect some laughter, some silence, along with anticipation that you're probably going to verbally nail Billy.

It is necessary to make the humor dignified, for otherwise Billy feels humiliated and the power struggle continues. The wise teacher says, "What I'd like to do is go to my car, drive to the airport, take a flight to Hawaii, get there, and lie in the sun so that I can relax. Then I wouldn't have to think or worry about it. But Billy is upset today, and he and I will need to deal with this later on. Today's lesson is . . . "

SITUATION

I would like to learn how to deal with the child in my after-school detention for minor discipline problems: excess chatter in class, bothering other students, bothering me, late papers, etc. It seems that if I give this child constant attention, he's okay in class for that day. As soon as I direct my attention to someone or something else, he acts out. I have repeated conversations with his parents about his need for all the attention given in class. They respond with, "We just don't know what to do with him." I have used rewards, which may work for a day, but that's about it. I have tried "plans" with him, but as soon as things start going smoothly he manipulates the situation for more attention. Help!

ANALYSIS/SOLUTION

In a preventive discipline sense, it is helpful to guess at identifying his basic needs. My guess is that "belonging," "power," and perhaps "competence" may be driving the behavior. The question becomes, "How can I teach while at the same time enabling this child to feel connected to others, have a sense of his own power, and feel successful?" As with all possibilities, there are no patented answers that will work every time. But I would consider finding a number of ways to positively "empower" him.

Perhaps he can be a room monitor, paper passer-outer, or line leader. I might empower him through problem solving. "I've noticed that when you are the center of attention in the class, you seem happiest. And I am going to try as hard as I can to help you be the center of attention. But sometimes, when you get up and start tapping the other kids or talking to them, I can't teach and they can't learn. What do you think you can do about that?" You might offer other suggestions as to how he can be helpful throughout the school (another way of empowering).

A sense of belonging can be enriched by brainstorming with the class some ways that classmates can reach out more directly for this student. You might say to the class, "I think that when Stuart talks and bothers others, that is his way of wanting to be friends. We all need friends. Any suggestions for Stuart as to how else he might make friends here?"

When students act in passive-aggressive ways, they are often expressing anger that they are afraid to express more directly. If this boy's behavior is also troublesome to his parents, who don't know what to do, then the family might benefit from counseling to get to some of the root causes of his behavior. When competence is at issue (i.e., late papers), children often need to be reassured that classroom success is best achieved by following the rules and putting forth effort. Be sure to emphasize his successes when you provide either verbal or written feedback.

Finally, it is quite possible that he enjoys your company and figures that in order to get it he has to act bad. Any children who repeatedly get detention are usually there because they want to be. Let him know that he does not have to act up to get some of your special time. In fact, you might surprise him by taking him for an ice cream after school one day.

BASIC NEEDS ACTIVITY

A discipline plan should include ways of addressing the basic needs that lead to discipline problems when ungratified. All children have a most primary need for survival. There are those who have not sufficient food or shelter. I therefore include that most basic need along with the five others noted in this chapter. Consider survival needs along with each of the five basic needs presented (capable/successful, caring/belonging, power/control, generosity/helping, stimulation/fun) and explore—either alone or preferably with a group of colleagues—ideas, strategies, and techniques for each. What are you comfortable doing? If you want your classroom to be more fun, how can you make it that way and still teach content? If you have a child who seems disconnected and unbonded, how will you seek to make contact?

DIRECTIONS

Brainstorm activities, classroom or school practices that are congruent with either meeting, maintaining, or enhancing each of these basic needs:

FEELING SUCCESSFUL / CAPABLE

FEELING CARED ABOUT / BELONGING

FEELING POWERFUL AND IN CONTROL

GIVING TO OTHERS / GENEROSITY

FEELING STIMULATED / HAVING FUN

GETTING MY SURVIVAL NEEDS MET

2

Principles of Effective Discipline

Most discipline programs incorrectly place their emphases upon strategies and techniques. The latest gimmick is offered to get Johnny to behave. The problem is that there are a lot of Johnnys out there, and not all respond according to how the text or technique says they should. Having worked with thousands of children and adults, I have concluded that it is fruitless to expect that any technique will work with all people who present the same symptom. Before prescribing treatment for a headache, the competent physician needs to get at the source of the problem. The same felt headache may reflect many different underlying problems in different people—stress, eye problems, migraine, fatigue, tumor. ∗ The competent teacher needs to get at the reasons or functions of a given maladaptive behavior to formulate a strategy likely to work.

By way of illustration, I am reminded of an elderly woman whom I saw at a group home for mentally retarded adults. She unexpectedly began having tantrums. Her tantrums were specific: she would remove her protective helmet (pre-scribed for a seizure disorder) and throw it at people. This was quite out of character, as she was normally a rather docile person. Since she lacked the language skill to articulate her problem(s), the staff could only guess what might be on her mind. They approached Al, the "expert." My first thought was that, in all the years of my work and writing, not once have I encountered the problem of what one should do for helmet throwing. Obviously, the most sensible immediate strategy would be to duck!

Since there was no ready-made technique or formula that fit this woman, I explored her behavior more carefully and learned that her brother, who was the one family member who maintained regular contact, had been sick and missing some of his visits. Furthermore, a staff member with whom she dined occasionally outside the residence had resigned within recent weeks. It was only after the woman had been reassured about her brother's health and another staff member began to go out to dinner with her that her agitation abated. It would have been missing the point if we had prematurely developed a strategy based only upon the problem behavior (e.g., reinforce her when she isn't throwing a helmet, use a time-out strategy when she is).

It will never be possible to compile a list of all possible techniques to be used when problem behaviors occur. Formulas sometimes fail to fit situations. It is therefore more important that educators be guided by a sound set of principles and guide-lines from which they can apply existing strategies or develop new ones.

1. Long-term behavior changes vs. short-term quick fixes. Many discipline problems limit their scope to the "what-to-do-when" situations. We have found that there is never any one thing that you can do with all children in all situations that will be effective. Any program that rigidly defines rewards, consequences, or punishments for all kids is doomed to failure. There is a plethora of examples of students who do not improve despite the provision of rewards following "desired" behavior. Some actually get worse when rewards are given. Some students do not respond with changed behavior when detentions and suspensions are given. In fact, some seem to seek these punishments. We can assume that that is the case when the same student keeps doing the same thing despite the consequence or punishment.

The quest for quick, short-term solutions to complex problems is an ongoing social problem that pervades all aspects of our culture. Because we can instantly turn on the TV, cook a meal in a microwave, call an 800 number and get a product overnight, charge anything we want to our credit cards, we tend to expect similiar rapid solutions to problems involving people. My brother, who is an attorney, was recently bemoaning the increasing use of the fax machine. He told me that he was planning to go on an anti-fax crusade. When I asked him why, he shared that it was common these days for his clients to expect immediate solutions. After all, if they could immediately get him the document, he should just as rapidly have the solution.

People take time! Dealing with discipline takes time. Children are not fax machines or credit cards. When they misbehave, they tell us that they need help in learning a better way. They are telling us that there are basic needs not being met that are motivating the behavior. If all we do is focus on what to do after the behavior has happened, we have only a choice of better and worse solutions. The best time to deal with behavior is *before* there are problems. Focusing on and addressing basic needs is time well spent. Preventing discipline problems from occurring is far preferable to dealing with them after the fact.

If you believe that dealing with discipline is part of the job, then you will give yourself enough time to plan for and deal with disruptive classroom situations in the most effective way both for the long and short term. You must bring the same professionalism, energy, and enthusiasm to discipline as you do to the content you teach. For some students, discipline *is* the content of their school lives. It is our belief that effective discipline really means teaching kids how to become responsible. Within that framework, discipline problems are viewed as an opportunity to teach responsibility. We believe that there are far too many children and adolescents who have little idea of what it really means to be responsible. They need to learn that they have choices and that they need to plan their behavior. They need someone who cares enough to engage them beyond tossing them out of the room, scolding them, or criticizing when they behave in irresponsible, perhaps outrageous, ways.

I have had frustrated teachers suggest that they should not have to put up with bad behavior. They say they are already overworked with demands to increase test performance and content competencies. They say they simply do not have the time to deal with difficult kids. It should be the administrator's or counselor's job to deal with these kids. My contention is that discipline is a job for everyone in the school when it is viewed as teaching kids how to be responsible. Long after kids forget facts, they will remember the people who most influenced them. Dealing with discipline gives us many opportunities to really affect a child's life.

As educators, we must maintain the proper perspective with regard to our priorities. Facts and content are forever changing. When I hear teachers tell me that they simply do not have the time to work on behavior, it occurs to me that they are missing the most important lessons to be taught. Facts change and can always be learned, but learning how to behave respectfully, nonviolently, and with proper social grace is much harder. It used to be that there was no doubt that Christopher Columbus discovered America. Now, there is debate as to whether it was Columbus or Leif Eriksson. Native Americans understandably take issue with either version. My son recently brought home his biology text, and, as I was scanning its contents, I came upon a photograph of the human pancreas. I began to read. What I learned that day is that today's version of the pancreas is quite different from the one that I learned in biology class 25 years ago. And 25 years from now, there will be knowledge of the pancreas that adds to and dispels currently-held truths about its functions. But 25 years from now, it will still be important for those seeking successful employment to know how to get along with others.

2. Stop doing ineffective things. We have all heard and used the expression "People are creatures of habit." This is why people continue to do things even after all of the feedback suggests that what we are doing is ineffective. With regard to discipline, some kids simply do not respond to "common-sense" or "empirically sound" strategies. There are children who get worse when they are positively reinforced. Some can be taught "social skills" and yet continue to misbehave. Others are sent to detention on what seems a daily basis, seeming neither to learn nor benefit from being there. We must stop doing ineffective things! Molnar and Lindquist (1989) point out that, when a solution either does not work or makes matters worse, probably the solution is itself part of the problem. Let go of doing things with either groups or individual students that are not effective.

We need to let go of our common-sense notions when we encounter people who do not respond in the "prescribed" fashion. In Chapter 6, and throughout the questions and cases sections of this book, there will be some suggestions, solutions, and interventions that can best be termed "unconventional."

I once worked with an autistic teenager who seemed locked into his own world most of the time. After a range of "behavior" methods were used unsuccessfully in efforts to get him to be more responsive, I observed that there was greater human contact made with him by first entering his world. When he sat rocking, I would sit across from him and rock. When he made facial grimaces, so too would I. We got to a point at which I could reach out my hand and he would grasp it, get up, and go for a walk with me. Together we would smell the flowers and enjoy the sunshine. By entering his world, I was affirming the validity of his existence. My attention was not dependent upon him behaving "appropriately." This had the paradoxical effect of making him want to more frequently join my world. By accepting people as they are, we make it possible for them to risk change.

Sam was a fifth-grader who did many things to create problems in his class. After Mrs. Jones had tried virtually every conventional strategy with little benefit, she was encouraged to think of the behavior that made her the most upset with Sam. She said that it was his physical aggression. She was asked to consider all of the positive attributes or personality characteristics one could associate with physical aggression. Being a nonviolent person, this was difficult for her. After much thought, she said, "People don't walk all over you . . . . You stand up for what you believe in . . . . Not taking any cr— from anyone." She then practiced a new way of communicating with Sam. Although physical aggression in the classroom cannot and should not be tolerated, she was ready to find a new, positive way to affirm Sam. She began to say such things as, "Sam, I really think it is important that you stick up for yourself, and when you fight, I know that's what you're doing. Fighting here is not okay, and, as you know, there are consequences. But keep sticking up for yourself. That's important. And if you'd like to get together and figure out some other ways to stick up for yourself without getting into trouble, I'll be happy to meet with you for as long as it takes."

Let's look at another example. Consider a student who is chronically late to class. For many students, a reminder to come on time, a phone call home, detention, an explanation of the importance of being on time, or a reward might effectively resolve this problem. All of the above might be considered "conventional" or common-sense interventions. But suppose that Sally is a student who has not changed her behavior despite these interventions. Sally and her teacher get into daily power struggles over her tardiness. Rather than continue to do ineffective things, Sally's teacher can decide to affirm her. She must suspend her belief in the primary importance of coming to class on time for Sally and instead seek behavior(s) that she can genuinely affirm. The next time Sally is late, Mrs. Long says, "Sally, as you know, I've been really angry with your lateness. Although I'd prefer that you come to class on time, the fact is that you participate very well when you are here and often have lots to share. Thanks for coming and contributing." Mrs. Long has moved the discussion beyond the issue of time to class and has found or rediscovered the primary importance of helping Sally realize that her value is more than whether or not she is punctual. Sally is much more likely to come to class on time.

The beliefs we hold about our capabilities influence our behavior. Changing behavior is a way of influencing those beliefs. Paradoxically, we are most likely to facilitate change when we respect someone's current views and behaviors, while providing sufficient safety and support as he explores other possibilities.

QUESTIONS

1. Think of a class or a student who did not or does not respond in the desired way to your "common-sense" interventions.

2. What are all of the things that you have done to try to change this?

3. Have you discussed this child or class with a colleague whom you respect in seeking other strategies?

4. Have you checked in with other educators who might be working with this child to assess who is having more success?

5. If the problem is about a child, which of the basic needs do you think is driving his misbehavior?

6. What are you doing to address those basic needs that you believe are responsible?

7. Is there anything about this child's behavior that you can appreciate? Perhaps you can even think about aspects of the misbehavior that can be respected but not tolerated in a classroom setting.

8. Practice making statements to the child, affirming him and the value of his behavior while setting necessary limits.

SITUATION

There is incessant talking and socializing among my seventh-graders that really interferes with instruction. I have set up rules, enforced consequences, and even expressed my frustration with the class, after which I invited them to come up with solutions to the problem, all to little or no avail. We might get one or two better days, but then the chatter returns. I am at the end of my rope.

ANALYSIS / SOLUTION

The principle "Stop doing ineffective things" applies in this situation. It sounds as if you have been reasonable in attempting to address this problem. It is possible that the disease of the decade, *boredom,* is contributing to this problem. You might therefore explore alternative teaching strategies with this group (e.g., cooperative learning) that enable them to learn and socialize simultaneously. Keep in mind that the number one thing that students of all ages say they want more of at school is time to be with their friends. Seventh grade is a peak age for peer contact. You might also consider implementing strategies that adhere to the philosophy of "legalizing misbehavior that you cannot stop." For example, you could acknowledge their need to socialize by saying:

"It looks as if catching up on the latest friend stuff is more important now than this science experiment. I can understand that. Sometimes I prefer to be with my friends rather than listening to someone trying to teach me something. So let's take the next three minutes and make sure that you talk to whomever you would like. When the time is up, we'll need to get busy working with no more talking."

You can even have fun doing this. You can say, "Okay, everybody, when I count to three, it'll be time for socializing. Ready . . . one . . . two . . . three . . . *socialize!*" By encouraging the behavior that is occurring anyway, and by putting some limits around it that are acceptable to you, you will often stop the behavior.

3. I will be fair, and I won't always treat everyone the same. Some who read Sally and Mrs. Long's brief scenario will take exception because you will be concerned about the disciplinary (or lack thereof) message to other kids. You may think that it is great to treat all kids as individuals, but the consequence of doing so may be that kids accuse you of being unfair. You worry that if you primarily focus on Sally's positive contributions, other kids are going to hear that they too can come late and feel that their teacher finds it acceptable. You want to avoid the following: "Mrs. Long, it isn't fair. You made me stay after school and you don't do nothin' to Sally."

Because "Discipline with Dignity" seeks to teach children how to be responsible, it is necessary to tailor the consequences to the child. Just as children need different approaches to reading, they need different approaches to discipline. It is necessary, however, that children be shown and taught the difference between being fair and treating everyone exactly the same way. Once they understand, you will be free to truly engage each child and do the best thing according to their needs.

We believe that being fair means giving each person what she needs, not treating everyone exactly the same. Equality means that all people are born of equal value, but, since no two people are identical, it is absurd to think that everyone should be treated exactly the same. Discipline codes that seek to "uniformly" or "consistently" do the same thing to all kids are doomed to failure. As educators, our priority is to teach students what they need to know. We must move beyond assembly-line strategies if we want students to compete in a high-tech workplace that values creativity, problem solving, and individual thought.

When we lock ourselves into doing the same thing to all kids no matter what, we actually wind up undermining discipline. We are forced into having to do things that we know will not work with a given student in order to preserve the "integrity" of the system. Worse, we may feel forced into doing something that may be dangerous to the child. For example, if a phone call home is the third consequence for all children in a class who do not do their homework, should the teacher call or not call those parents who have a short fuse and tendency toward abuse? Is there value to withholding a field trip to the zoo from a child who hates animals? Will a student really seek to avoid future detentions if he sees that time after school as an opportunity for peace, quiet, help with work, or special nurturance from the teacher?

What does it say about a discipline program if the sixth consequence on the list is the one that will be most effective with a given youngster but the teacher feels obligated to use the first five ineffective ones? "Joey, I know that consequence six will really work best for you, but because the system is the same for everyone, I'll do five useless things with you first." Doesn't that sound ridiculous? Does it make any instructional sense? Would a competent teacher tell some of her third-graders, "The second-grade teacher told me that you guys don't learn to read well with phonics. But we'll do phonics anyway for the first three months, and if you still don't learn, we'll do something else that will probably work better."

Being fair but not treating everyone the same allows you to have a foundation of rules based upon sound values for *everyone*. Specific consequences are implemented on an *individual* basis so that each child can learn a better way based upon her actions, beliefs, and needs. We advocate having clear and specific rules, with each having several possible consequences from which you, the teacher, can choose those that are most likely to best teach the child. Programs or systems that dictate how all teachers will react and what they will do sacrifice professionalism for "equality." They seek to make their program "teacher-proof," or, colloquially, "foolproof," which condescendingly implies that even a teacher can do it.

In *Discipline with Dignity,* we offered the following as an example of a way to teach students the difference between fair and equal:

> *Ask your students to imagine 10 patients waiting for their turn to see the doctor. One has a cold, one has a broken arm, one has pneumonia, one has poison ivy, one has a sprained ankle, one has diarrhea, one has allergies, one has chickenpox, one has a splinter and another came in for an annual checkup. All of a sudden, the doctor comes out and announces that today is aspirin day. All patients will be treated equally and given aspirin to solve their ailments.*

A lively discussion can now ensue analyzing whether the doctor is being fair, although he is clearly being equal.

SITUATION

I get really annoyed when parents complain about discipline. They expect the same treatment for everybody and are always quick to point out when their little darlin' got it worse than some other kid. I've been doing a lot of the "Discipline with Dignity" methods for a few years, and they are for the most part very effective, but I sure have trouble at times with parents about the "fair and not equal" part.

ANALYSIS / SOLUTION

The best way we have found to handle this is to avoid getting caught up in defensive posturing. You will discover this the minute you find yourself talking about actions other than those directed toward the complaining parents' child. First, please keep being fair and not equal. Next, be preventive with this practice by sharing your discipline program with parents verbally and in writing. Let them know that, like a good doctor, you seek consequences that teach each child a better, more responsible way.

Finally, when you are accused of being unfair or unequal, do two things. First, thank the parent for being concerned about her child and acknowledge that there may be better ways of teaching this child responsibility. Share the differences between consequences and punishments by letting the parent know why you chose the consequence that you did and how you believe that will best help this particular child learn to better follow a rule. Stay open to hearing a more effective way from the parent. Next, refuse to discuss your actions concerning any other child with the parent. Remind the parent that you really are not at liberty to discuss another child except to say that you attempt to teach each child according to what you believe will be the best way for her to learn. You might even say something on the order of, "Please don't expect me to treat your child exactly like any other, because your child is special in her own way. I think too much of her to simply view her as the same as everyone else. Now, if you can help me figure a better way to work with your child, I would love to learn. But please don't expect me to either talk about other children or to necessarily treat your child as I would any other."

I have found that most parents' anger can be easily defused when this message is given with genuineness and sincerity. They leave knowing that their child is viewed as a unique person, and they can feel confident that you do not gossip about one child or family to another.

4. Rules must make sense. There are many reasons that people break rules, but one that seems universally true is that rules viewed as stupid are the least likely to be followed. Observation of any highway in America provides proof. Rare is the highway that does not have several speeders at a given time.

The same is true for "speed traps." These are generally 35-mph zones of open-spaced roads with rarely another car or person in sight. Although it makes no "sense" for that to be the speed limit, the police are all too willing to stake out those spots and await the unwary driver doing a sensible 50. Rules in schools must not be traps that await the unwary student. Rather, they should be the guidelines needed in order for success to happen.

There are many instances in which students are made servants of the rules rather than the rules being there to serve students. Students need to see how a rule benefits them. A student who sees little value in doing homework is unlikely to do it unless she can see how she will benefit by doing a particular assignment or unless she has a long-term goal of achieving well at school. There are some students who will continue to wear hats to school unless they can see that there are learning or life benefits either to themselves or others from not wearing a hat. Walkman™ radios will be listened to by students for whom quiet makes no sense.

Students need and deserve an explanation for why things are the way they are. If you find yourself telling students that your rules exist because "That's the way it's always been," "Rank has its privileges," "Someday you'll understand," or "Because I said so," you are depriving them of an opportunity to learn that education trains people to think. You become the enemy who extorts compliance through fear and will be targeted for either direct or "terrorist" attack.

QUESTIONS

1. Think of rules in your life that you feel forced to live by. How do you deal with these?

2. Think of the rules in your school. How do these benefit kids?

3. If I were a kid and asked why it is of benefit for me to come to a class that I hate, see no value in, am forced to attend, or in which I am seen as a failure, what would I say? If some students feel that way in your class, why should they behave?

4. Which rules in your school exist to serve kids?

5. Which rules in your school do you think make kids feel that they are servants?

6. How could you best find out which rules make sense and which do not to the students?

5. Model what you expect. Like most things having to do with learning and human interactions, actions speak louder than words. What you do as a teacher and, more important, how you do it, are much more powerful than what you tell students they should do. Birdwhistell's research found that 60% of how we come across is determined by body language. Between 30% and 35% is associated with tone of voice, while only 5% to 10% of the meaning of the message is the message itself.

Let your students see you living by the same code of behavior that you expect of them. If you assign homework, be sure to promptly do your own homework by getting their work back to them as quickly as possible. Our research and observations indicate that if assignments are not returned, students lose interest in doing them. When they are returned late (more than three days after they are turned in), the only students who benefit are those who care about their grades, because there is rarely any learning from mistakes that occur following that interval.

Be visible in the halls between classes as a message of safety and security to your kids. Speak to them in a way that you want them to speak to you. When conflict occurs, let them see you implement solutions that are respectful, nonviolent, and verbally nonaggressive. If you want to promote friendliness among your students, have a smile on your face as you greet them into the room. Teach the real, healing value of apologizing by saying you are sorry to a student when you lose your temper or otherwise blow it. In short, let them see you as a model of how you want them to be.

QUESTIONS

1. List each rule that you have for your students.

2. Do you hold yourself accountable for following all of these rules?

3. What do you think are the consequences of having a rule for students but not for teachers?

4. What practices do you currently use to model your expectations of students?

5. What would you be willing to do that would bring your own behavior more in line with what you expect of your students?

6. If you gave your students a chance to make some rules for you, what do you think they would do?

6. Responsibility is more important than obedience. Earlier in this book, we discussed the problems and limitations of subscribing to an obedience model of discipline. In short, obedience means, "Do as you are told . . . . Do as I tell you whether or not you agree." Obedience methods are ineffective and may be dangerous to the user. Consider the case of a high school student who pulled a gun on a male teacher who had threatened him with the warning, "Behave or else." When the student produced the weapon and replied, "Or else what?" the teacher quickly backed off and the student put the gun away and returned to his seat (as reported in the Newark *Sunday Star Ledger,* October 21, 1991).

Obedience means do not question and certainly do not be different. Obedience always implies a hierarchical structure in which one or a small group of the powerful dictates the terms of behavior for the masses. History clearly reveals much misery among the masses under this form of government. The seeds of retaliation and rebellion are invariably sown when people feel robbed of their personal freedom to make choices. The major tools of obedience models of discipline are rewards and punishments.

Responsibility means, *Make the best decision you possibly can with the information you have available.* Within a responsibility model of discipline, it is necessary for children to accumulate information, see the options available to them, learn to anticipate consequences, and then choose the path that they feel is in the best interest of themselves and others. Because learning to be responsible is an ongoing, dynamic process, bad decisions are viewed as opportunities by which children can learn to make better ones. The processes by which children increase their competence in learning responsibility are the same ones used to teach internal locus of control (see p.13)—increased awareness, choosing, planning, and predicting.

"Obedience" is not always bad. In fact, there are elements of the "do-as-you-are-told" philosophy that are *essential* in order for a civilized society to survive, such as when danger is an issue. It would be entirely irresponsible for a parent to allow her toddler to touch a hot frying pan in order to learn of its danger. The police are needed when assaults are threatened or occur at school. When speed and safety are factors, techniques that promote obedience are required.

It is irresponsible and naïve for educators to believe that they can facilitate a change in behavior among hardened, anti-social, and angry youth simply by offering more love, caring, and opportunities for decision making. In my work with "behaviorally disordered" and "juvenile-delinquent" youth, a combination of obedience and responsibility methods is need-ed for growth and change to occur. Conventional behavioral methods that are obedience-oriented ("Do as I say and you will be rewarded or punished") are often required in the early stages for such youth to feel a sense of safety and security (someone else will put controls to the impulses that I cannot). Unfortunately, most programs never proceed beyond this. Many children who have not been taught to behave responsibly may learn to behave well when they are being monitored. When the authority figure is not present, they often return to old, familiar behaviors. As they get older, they have more and more trouble responding to situations in which they are on their own. They become depen-dent on what the voice of authority demands. "Obedient" chil-dren listen to the authority that has the loudest, most persuasive voice. In far too many instances, that "voice" is the television, stereo, Nintendo™ game, peers, or even the neighborhood drug dealer.

We must develop discipline techniques that move beyond obedience. We must ask ourselves questions larger than "Does it work?" We must consider such things as:

(a) What happens later?

(b) What happens to motivation for learning?

(c) How does the discipline method affect self-esteem?

(d) What happens to an individual's dignity?

(e) How would we (the instructor) be affected if we were at the receiving end of the method?

Most students do not need any kind of systematic discipline method in order to behave. We have found that approximately 80% of all kids will behave well and will respond with improved behavior to *either* good or bad methods of discipline. We have also found that approximately 5% of all students chronically misbehave and that they generally respond very poorly to most known conventional forms of discipline. About 15% of the student population fence-sits. These kids break rules on a somewhat regular basis. They do not blindly accept the classroom principles, and they fight the restrictions. Their motivation and achievement ranges from completely on to completely off, from high to low, and is affected by influences such as what happened at home that morning, how they perceive the classroom activity, the teacher's behavior toward them, or their current status needs from others. These students need a clear set of expectations and consequences. If they are not given enough structure, they can disrupt learning for all the other students.

The goal of a good discipline plan is to provide structure and control for the 15% without alienating or overly regulating the 80% and without backing the 5% into a corner. Programs that are too heavily obedience-oriented give the illusion of success because they may provide short-term control of the 15%. In such schools and classrooms, however, seeds are sown for them and the out-of-control students to explode in rebellion and for many of the 80%ers to lose interest in learning.

QUESTIONS

1. Make a list of the discipline techniques you use. Do they teach children to make decisions or to do as they are told?

2. Responsibility means "making the best decision you can." Can you think of times when you, the teacher, have acted "responsibly" by not obeying?

3. How would you feel about students doing what they think is right, not necessarily what they are told?

4. How often do you encourage students to make choices about their own behavior? How often do you tell them what to do?

5. Think of a student whom you have frequently told what to do but with poor response. What do you think might happen if you stopped telling the student what to do and how to do it?

6. Think of dangerous situations that threaten the safety of others or the maintenance of property. Fights, carrying of weapons, and destruction of property will probably come to mind. List these things. Behaviors in this category need to have very clear rules and a rapid, no-nonsense approach that falls within the category of "obedience" models of discipline. What are some rewards or punishments that are necessary in order to deal effectively with these behaviors and that do not humiliate the student?

7. Think of all other behaviors pertaining to discipline that may be annoying, irritating, bothersome, or in conflict with your preferences but that are destructive of neither others nor property. List as many of these as you can think of. Consider how you may help students who display such behaviors through increased awareness, predicting, planning, or choosing to become more responsible for their own behavior by making better choices.

SITUATION

The case of Zachariah Toungate, an eight-year-old who attends the Mina Elementary School in Basrop, Texas, has received a lot of attention. Zachariah refused to have his rattail cut off and was therefore judged to be in violation of the school's discipline code. Zach has been isolated from his classmates and forced to learn in "solitary confinement," a small room in which he is tutored in his subjects. School officials have stated that Zach is welcome to return to his class just as soon as he complies with the code. At this point, the case is before the courts. How would "Discipline with Dignity" handle this situation?

ANALYSIS / SOLUTION

This case gets right to the heart of a key principle that drives the "Discipline with Dignity" approach. This principle says that "responsibility is more important than obedience." We define obedience as following rules without question, regardless of philosophical beliefs, ideas of right and wrong, instincts and experiences, or values. A student "does it" because he is told to do it. In the short term, obedience can offer educators relief, a sense of power and control, and an oasis from the constant bombardment of defiance. In the long run, however, obedience leads to student immaturity, a lack of responsibility, an inability to think clearly and critically, and a feeling of helplessness. The consequences are withdrawal, aggressiveness, and power struggles. There are times during which an obedience model of discipline is appropriate: when safety is at stake. Aggressive classroom or school behavior needs to be dealt with in a no-nonsense, authoritative way. Certainly, "time-out" and "in-school suspension" (the school's primary means of isolating disruptive students) may have a place during these times, especially when students are expected to develop a plan for better future behavior. These techniques may enable students and staff to reflect upon why they did what they did and, more important, what they can and will do the next time similar circumstances occur. Unfortunately, too often such methods are used to wear away at a student's resistances in hopes that he will obey.

We have found that rules and policies need to make sense. Kids need to understand how a rule benefits either themselves or others. The rules that are most likely to be broken by the greatest number of people are those that make the least sense. If you cannot see how a rule specifically benefits either individuals or groups, and if, when asked by a student, "Why do we have that rule?" the best you can say is, "Because I told you so," or "Because those are the rules," then it is undoubtedly a poor rule, which does little more than frustrate those who have to follow it.

We have trouble seeing how Zachariah Toungate's behavior either interferes with his learning or that of others. An individual's behavior must have a tangibly negative effect upon others in order for it to be considered a discipline problem. Zachariah's rattail would appear to affect no one other than him. If the school authorities are concerned about his influence upon others, then they should be prepared to show how rattails adversely affect achievement, behavior, the development of solid values, or all of the above. If the school authorities believe that making Zach comply is a way to show kids the importance of living by the rules of society, then we say that a democratic society's rules need to make sense or they should not exist.

Only when student safety is at risk can we see the benefits of a dress or perhaps hair code. For example, a rule requiring school uniforms with no jewelry in a school within an impoverished community sends a powerful signal to the community that the focus of this school is on learning and not on street ways of making money. Schools should be about teaching kids how to be responsible: decision making, developing effective plans, and becoming thinking, caring citizens.

7. **Always treat students with dignity.** This is perhaps the most important of all the principles, because without dignity students learn to hate school and learning. When we attack students' dignity, we might get them to follow the rules but we lose them to anger and resentment. Discipline techniques must be compatible with helping students maintain or enhance their self-esteem. Methods that attack dignity are generally those that include put-downs, sarcasm, criticism, scolds, and threats that are delivered publicly. It is easier to treat "good" kids with dignity, although all too often even they feel discounted, ignored, and put down by important adults. Listening to what a student thinks, being open to feedback from students, using I-messages to communicate your feelings to them, explaining why you want something done a certain way and how that will likely be of benefit to the student, and giving students some say in classroom affairs are all ways of communicating dignity to them. The message is: you are important.

It is indeed difficult to be dignified with students who tell you where to go and how to get there! Because we are human, it is understandable that, when our buttons are pressed, we react from the gut. Yet it is precisely during these moments that displays of dignity become all the more necessary for a number of reasons. The student who attacks needs to learn non-attacking ways of dealing with stress. You can truly be a teacher in the purest sense by modeling alternatives during your own stressful moments with the student. Further, if you attack back, then escalation results and the power struggle simply gets worse. It is important that other students see you as capable and strong without being brutal when your or their well-being is disrupted. They need to realize that there are alternatives to full-scale warfare even after the first bomb has been dropped.

"Discipline with Dignity" encourages teachers and other caregivers to be aware of how they communicate their expectations that students correct their behavior. Dignity in discipline can often be accomplished by using privacy, eye contact, and proximity when you need to deliver a corrective message to a student. Make your comments quietly so that only you and the student can hear, with eye contact (being sensitive to possible cultural or emotional issues regarding eye contact), and in close physical proximity. We have seen many potentially explosive situations prevented with Privacy, Eye contact, and Proximity (P.E.P.).

QUESTIONS

1. Can you think of any interventions that you experienced as a child in school that attacked your dignity? What effect(s) did that have on your behavior? Motivation to learn? Self-esteem?

2. Can you remember any teachers who were able to get across to you that there was a better way to behave? How did they approach you and communicate that to you?

3. Kids who regularly break rules often have low self-esteem because their dignity has been attacked along the way. In your class, are there ways for such students to feel hope, to see themselves as competent and feel empowered? What can you do to create these possibilities in your class?

CRITERIA FOR USING A DISCIPLINE METHOD

It is our belief (Curwin and Mendler) that, for a discipline method to be considered effective for both the short term and long term, it must meet the following criteria:

1. It must work to stop disruptive behavior and/or build constructive, prosocial behavior.

2. You (the teacher) would find the method acceptable if you were on the receiving end. Use yourself and your feelings as a guide to the relative emotional benefits or liabilities of any and all methods.

3. The methods are geared toward teaching responsibility (better decision making) even when obedience is necessary (e.g., safety).

4. You are willing to model the method, not merely preach it.

5. You can identify and explain how following a rule or procedure can provide both immediate and long-term benefits.

6. The method is compatible with the seven Principles of Effective Discipline.

3

The Process
of Change

IN MOST INSTANCES, the problem of discipline is conceptualized as a student who does something wrong in the classroom or some other place at school. An explicit or implicit rule has been broken and the student has interfered with the teaching-learning process. Action is viewed as necessary so that order can be restored. In most cases, the actions taken are done to or with the student with the expectation that the student will change her behavior so that it is more appropriate. Detention, suspension, time-out, reminders, warnings, and action plans are some of these methods. All share in common the belief that it is the student who must change in order for things to get better. The expectation that it is the student who must change is referred to as *inside-out* change. All methods that teach responsibility by furthering one's internal locus of control are inside-out methods. A student's plan represents what she will do differently to avoid future difficulty. The onus of responsibility for change rests squarely and exclusively with the student.

It is important that we broaden our picture of the change process to see that change occurs in ways other than exclusively expecting different behavior from the student. In fact, change can occur by mobilizing forces outside of the student so that these forces influence the student's decision making. Figure I provides an illustration of the change process.

In the middle of the central circle is the student who exhibits problem behavior. In each circle around the student are others with whom that student frequently interacts—the teacher, other students, school support people, community folks such as the preacher, and family members. Change in any of the small circles toward the difficult student may influence that student's decision making. I call that the *outside-in* change process: forces from the outside influencing change. Some effective discipline methods and strategies have a primarily outside-in dimension. Teachers can greet the difficult student, teach to the primary learning style, and use I-messages assertively and respectfully to influence changed behavior. Another way to facilitate change is by helping other students change their reactions to the student's difficult behavior. Change may also occur through affiliating the student with a Big Brother from the community, promoting strength and health within the family structure and encouraging stronger bonds (perhaps an older brother or sister needs to become more involved in working with a sibling), or bringing in other school support personnel to provide counseling, support, and other needed interventions.

Look at an example of how change can be approached both from the inside-out and from the outside-in, at times even simultaneously. Ken is an eight-year-old who verbally puts

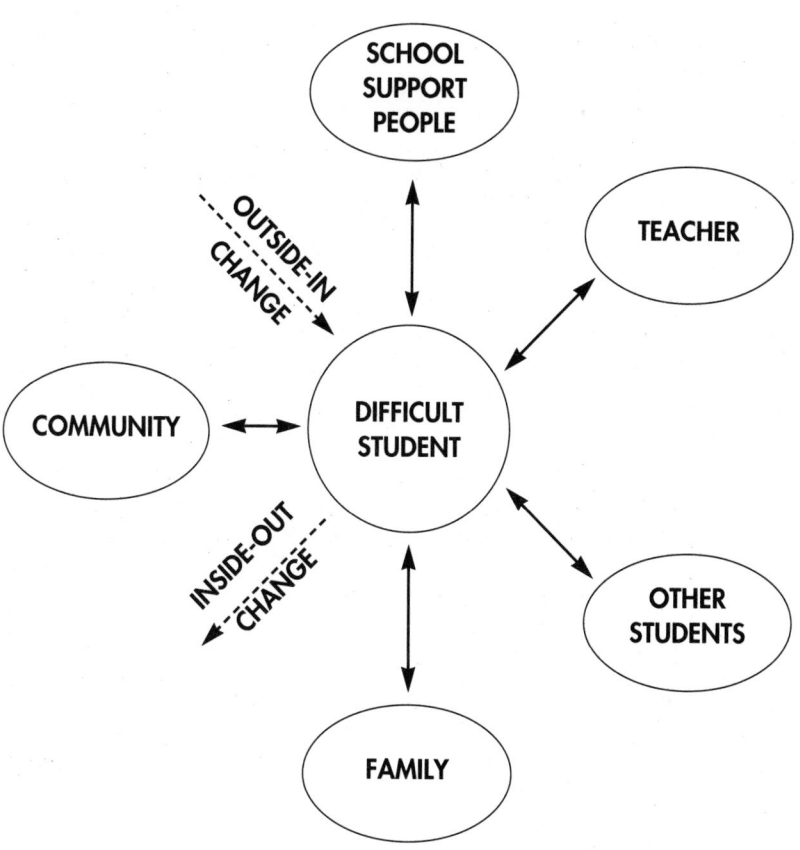

FIGURE I: THE CHANGE PROCESS

down his peers and is often aggressive toward them, especially on the playground. *Inside-out* change may occur by having Ken see the counselor so that he will become more aware of the triggers for his anger, having him attend a social-skills-building class to learn alternative ways of making friends, or developing a plan for future playground behavior without the aggression, along with staying after school to practice the plan. *Outside-in* change might be faciliated by helping the other students see that Ken's aggression could be a bid for friendship, and through problem-solving about ways they might reach out to him and what they can do other than put him down when he gets angry. The teacher might sense that Ken has unmet needs for power and belonging and is out of touch with generosity, so she can put him in charge of some classroom responsibilities, make him a line leader, and talk to the kindergarten teacher about Ken's becoming a helper in that room. A community Big Brother may be sought for some mentoring. Family members can learn to better understand the origin of Ken's problems and, we might hope, be part of the solution.

"Three-Dimensional Discipline" is the term that Curwin and I have used for many years to describe the various strategies and methods connected to Discipline with Dignity. Three-Dimensional Discipline provides a system for implementing a discipline policy that is consistent with the needs of the teacher and the students. When the plan is implemented on a classroom level, each teacher and group of students is involved in developing the plan. When the plan is designed for individuals or small groups, some or all of the groups identified in Figure I may be mobilized to assist the change process. When a schoolwide approach such as behavior in the cafeteria or halls, on the playground, or in the auditorium is developed, representatives of each school role group, including administrators, teachers, students, and parents are involved. The three dimensions of discipline are:

1. The Prevention Dimension. This includes any and all of the strategies and methods that actively prevent discipline problems from occurring. Most methods associated with meeting the basic needs of students fall within this category. Also included are ways to deal with the stress associated with classroom disruptions. The prevention of discipline problems includes such concepts and strategies as:

(a) Effective teaching practices

(b) Ways to stimulate interest and motivate students

(c) Strategies to meet basic needs

(d) Non-harmful ways of expressing stress in the school setting

(e) Collaborative development of rules and consequences with students

(f) Matching teaching methods to diverse learning and intellectual styles

(g) Effective communication skills such as I-messages and active listening

2. The Action Dimension. Despite the best efforts of educators, there are times in which rules will be broken. The Action Dimension includes those strategies that are best used after discipline problems occur and that (a) put a halt to the misbehavior and (b) do it in a way that maintains both teacher and student dignity. Included are methods used immediately, during class time or in the hall when confronted by student misbehavior. The use of privacy, eye contact, and proximity (P.E.P.) when enforcing consequences provides an example of what is done when things move to the level of the action dimension.

3. The Resolution Dimension. As noted earlier, our observations suggest that in most schools approximately 5% of the school population accounts for about 95% of the serious or chronic misbehaviors. Simply stated, there are some students who come to school every day, but who either cannot or will not behave in an acceptable manner. Furthermore, some such students do not respond to conventional approaches that are both effective and appropriate with most other children. The Resolution Dimension offers a series of primarily unconventional strategies that are more apt to be both effective and affirming of the difficult-to-reach student.

Conventional and unconventional methods of discipline can be effective in different situations. All of the strategies and suggested methods fit into one or more of the three discipline dimensions (prevention, action, resolution) and change process paradigm (inside-out or outside-in). For a more extensive treatment of the theory and background associated with the three dimensions of discipline, the interested reader is referred to earlier works by Curwin and Mendler.

Effective Classroom Methods of Discipline

D ISCIPLINE IS MOST EFFECTIVE when each school and classroom has a discipline plan that defines its rules and
consequences. Each plan should reflect the attitudes,
needs, and preferences of the individuals involved. The tradi-
tional approach to discipline has been for adults in positions of
authority to outline all of the rules and consequences for children. That approach is rooted in the Obedience Model and will
at most be followed well by children who respect authority.
Children who do not respect the teacher's authority, who see little practical value to school, or who have no interest in following rules are unlikely to behave even when specific rules and
consequences are established.

For several years, teachers and schools have been implementing what Curwin and Mendler refer to as a "social contract," which seeks to involve students and teachers together as

partners in the discipline plan. When schoolwide discipline is involved, a cross-section of teachers, parents, students, and administrators work together to create policies. The essential elements for creating a social contract are:

1. A spirit of cooperation between teacher and students

2. A statement of principles that serve as the foundation for rules

3. Clear and specific rules

4. Method(s) for student involvement

5. Consequences that teach children better behavior

GENERATING A SPIRIT OF COOPERATION

There are many ways for administrators and teachers to teach children that the school belongs to them. Professionals are there to serve the needs of the children. Without children, there could not be any schools. It is necessary for development of character and self-esteem that children feel invited to become problem-solving partners with adults. The prevailing attitude in the classroom needs to be, "This is our classroom, and we are all responsible for what goes on here. There are many decisions and choices that we will need to make together throughout the year. These decisions include questions such as where we sit, how we line up, when we do different skills, which jobs each student has, what we can and cannot do when we feel angry, upset, or frustrated." The main factors that can help convey this spirit to children are the teacher's beliefs and openness.

PRINCIPLES

When teachers are asked to display or describe their rules, I often hear such things as, "Be prepared . . . . Be courteous . . . . Treat others as you wish to be treated . . . . Solve problems peacefully . . . . Show respect . . . . Listen when others are talking." These are general statements, not rules. They are essential as part of the discipline plan because general statements such as these provide the foundation upon which rules are developed. *Principles* are these essential general statements based upon values and attitudes that cannot be enforced by themselves. Like the Constitution and the Bill of Rights, they provide the guiding philosophy, values, and reasons for why we do things the way we do.

Principles should provide the reason(s) for the rules and the motivation for following rules. "Protection of people and property" is the reason for a speed limit. A slow speed limit is more likely to be followed when people know that there is a mountainous curve ahead or children playing. "Being safe at school" provides the motivation for allowing no weapons and expecting children to keep their hands and feet to themselves. The most effective school, classroom, and home rules are those built upon a solid foundation of principles.

The outstanding organization for educators, Phi Delta Kappa, has published a "garden" of values, which I see as an example of *principles.*

THE PDK GARDEN

In my garden I would first plant five rows of peas:
>Preparedness,
>Promptness,
>Perseverance,
>Politeness, and
>Prayer.

Next to them I would plant three rows of squash:
>Squash gossip,
>Squash criticism, and
>Squash indifference.

Then I would put in three rows of lettuce:
> Let us be faithful,
> Let us be loyal, and
> Let us love one another.

No garden is complete without turnips:
> Turn up for meetings,
> Turn up with a smile,
> Turn up with a new idea, and
> Turn up with determination.

—Anonymous

QUESTIONS

1. What values, beliefs, or attitudes are you trying to promote in your classroom? (I want students to. . . feel safe, achieve as well as they can, be courteous to each other, solve problems peacefully.)

2. Why do you want each one?

3. How will each make the classroom a better place?

4. Which of your beliefs are most congruent with those of the school and/or community?

5. Are there some beliefs (values) you hold that seem devalued by others? What are they? Can you think of ways to promote your point of view without attacking one that may be diametrically opposed? What ways can several perspectives peacefully co-exist?

6. If you work in a street-tough community where fighting is viewed as acceptable, how can your desire for peaceful solutions in the classroom become harmonious with the community attitude?

RULES

Since principles are necessarily vague in order to encompass a set of beliefs, they are not sufficient by themselves to promote effective discipline. Rules are needed that are clear, specific, and enforceable. There should be no doubt as to whether they have been broken or followed. They are the equivalent of laws that define acceptable and unacceptable behavior. The criteria for a good rule are:

1. It is clear and specific.

2. One can always tell whether or not the rule is broken or followed.

3. It makes sense to the people who enforce and receive it.

4. It states what is allowed as well as what is not allowed.

5. It is stated simply and demonstrated so that all can understand.

The following are examples of clear and specific rules. Notice how they tell students what they can do as well as what they cannot:

1. Keep your hands and feet to yourself.

2. Be prepared with books, pencils, and paper.

3. You may tell others when you are angry or you can take yourself to the "cool-off" corner, but you may not hit.

4. If someone is doing something you do not like, first ask him to stop before you tell the teacher.

One problem for some teachers is that, if they get too specific, then they will need too many rules. It is possible, and undesirable, to establish hundreds of rules in order to cover every anticipated problem behavior. For example, if a rule is to keep hands and feet to oneself and a student shoots a spitball, technically he has not violated the rule unless it has been specifically determined in advance. Spitballs come from the mouth, not the hands or feet. There may be one or a handful of students who challenge rules on this basis—"You can't do anything to me because there is no rule about spitballs." Rather than worry about accounting for every possibility, you, the teacher, should define those rules that are most important to you to run a safe environment, conducive to learning.

When minor, unanticipated things happen, you need to use sound judgment and good communication skills to deal with the problem at hand. In effect, all teachers need both *formal rules,* which define important expectations, and *informal rules,* which are not written and are implemented on a case-by-case basis. With the student who shoots spitballs, the teacher would be advised to informally enforce a rule by approaching the student and telling the student to stop. If certain behaviors continue to occur despite informal intervention(s), then a formal rule can be developed.

Rule effectiveness can be enhanced by demonstrating what rules look like when they are broken and followed. We advise that you role-play with your classes to show them what you mean by "keeping hands and feet to self" or "coming to class on time" or "raising your hand before speaking during group discussion," etc. We must realize that there are children and adolescents who may not share your notions about behavior. We have to move beyond simply telling students what we want by demonstrating the specifics we want them to practice.

I worked with a second-grade teacher who spent parts of the first two weeks of school practicing lining up and walking through the halls as a class. This wound up saving her much time later because she did not have to enforce consequences with children who did not understand or had no practice following the rule.

QUESTIONS

1. What rules do you feel you must have in order for good teaching and learning to occur in your classroom?

   (a)

   (b)

   (c)

   (d)

2. What principles provide the foundation for each of these rules? (e.g., Principle: "Be Respectful" . . . . Rule: If you have a suggestion to make the class better, wait until a private time to tell the teacher.)

3. What behaviors are likely to occur at your grade level that may need "informal" intervention(s)? Practice informal intervention(s) by using clear, firm, and respectful language that states *which* behaviors you find objectionable, *how* you feel, and *what* you want.

   A few examples:

   (a) When you come late to class, I feel upset because my teaching is interrupted. I'd like to see you here on time.

   (b) Food is for eating, not for throwing.

(c) Tapping pencils is distracting to me and others. Thanks for stopping.

Now you try it:

(a)

(b)

(c)

METHODS FOR STUDENT INVOLVEMENT AS RULE MAKERS

For several years, Curwin and Mendler have advocated including students as rule makers to create a classroom partnership. When teachers alone define all of the rules and consequences, a top-down, authoritarian system is established, with the students having no ownership in the classroom. When the system belongs exclusively to the teacher, the teacher alone has to enforce all of the consequences. When students act as rule makers and help define the standards, they have more interest in ensuring that the system works. They become more involved in monitoring their own and classmates' behavior so that problems are often resolved without directly involving the teacher. This saves much time in the instructional process.

We also believe that the best way of teaching children responsibility is to give them the opportunity to be responsible. There is no better way to teach responsibility than to involve students in decisions that will directly affect their lives. Three optional methods of involving students in the discipline plan are:

1. Students develop rules for the teacher. This option invites students to formulate rules or guidelines that they want their teacher to follow. It is perhaps the most controversial of the methods because many teachers are understandably reluctant to hand power over to students. We have found, however, a paradoxical relationship between sharing power and having more. When we empower others, we tend to receive more authority and respect. Be prepared for students to have noticed most, if not all, of your foibles and to address these in the form of rules. These rules generally address standard complaints about teachers' behavior. In my interviews with students, the things they say bother them most about their teachers are:

1. Asking us to read orally in front of the class

2. Telling us to get to class on time, but sometimes coming late yourself after talking with another teacher

3. Always blaming the same kids

4. Calling on the same person all of the time

5. Making us write things a hundred times

6. Talking during assembly or fire drill when we can't

7. Not showing us how to do something and then giving us homework

8. Name-calling

9. Punishing the whole class for the actions of a few

10. Telling us not to run in the halls but that we have to get there quickly

11. Yelling or embarrassing us in the class

12. Giving homework and then not correcting it or waiting forever to correct it

Students really enjoy making rules for their teacher. They love permission to identify their teacher's imperfections. When the teacher receives this feedback lightly and non-defensively, all can have some good laughs. When the teacher makes some changes, that empowers students in a very positive way.

If you are reluctant, limit students to two or three rules that most of the class want. Finally, any rule that violates a school rule or law, or that strongly goes against your values, or that is likely to make teaching in your style impossible, can be eliminated by your veto. If you invite students to develop rules for you, then it must be with a genuine spirit of cooperation. You must show a willingness to be flexible. Enforcing rules broken by the teacher should be with a reminder given privately by one or two students (a responsibility that can be rotated among the students).

2. Students develop rules for each other. You can let the students develop rules (and possibly consequences) for one another. The questions are, "In this class, how would you like each other to behave? What do you need from each other for this to be a good class?" Students can collaborate in small groups to generate a list of rules. You can collect the lists, eliminate duplicates, and put each one up for consensus. Only those rules favored by at least 70% of the class become part of the class contract. We identify this percentage because rules should not be popularity contests. The goal of this process is to have a strong program of discipline that adequately reflects the views of most students.

3. Students vote on negotiable rules. We have found that younger children who have had little if any experience as rule- or decision makers need a little more structure. This option asks the teacher to generate a list of "flag" (non-negotiable) rules and "negotiable" rules. The teacher explains the "flag" rules to the children. These are the necessary rules that have to do with safety, preparedness, and the like. The teacher then identifies other rules that are not necessary but that she thinks the children might want. These may be about the teacher's behavior or procedural rules having to do with who lines up first and which children get to clean the blackboard. For example, the teacher can tell her children that when she was a child she remembers wanting teachers who would smile in the morning, talk quietly, and make sure to say at least one nice thing to each child every day. She then asks how many children in the class want her to behave according to each of these standards.

Since having written *Discipline with Dignity,* a fourth method of student involvement has been developed:

4. Teacher defines the principles and students develop the rules. In this method, the teacher first lets students know which principles are most important to him/her in having a safe, enthusiastic environment that is most conducive to learning. The next step is for the students to develop specific rules connected to each of the principles. The teacher begins by letting students know that the class needs (1) a *safe* environment that (2) values *courtesy* and that (3) finds *respectful* ways of disagreeing with each other and solving disputes. Students are then invited in small groups to generate some rules that will make the class safe, courteous, and respectful. They are taught the criteria for a "good rule."

Discipline that involves students is more effective and more time-consuming in a preventive sense. It takes longer to involve students as partners than it does to simply announce how things are going to be. Obviously, the goal is to put more time in before there are problems so that fewer problems occur and less time is necessary to deal with them. This has been the experience of the thousands of teachers who have used this, or adaptations of this, approach. Because so many students enter and leave the classroom during the year (it is rare to find teachers who end the year with the same group of students with whom they began), the classroom contract needs to be regularly updated so that the rules continue to reflect the needs of the individuals that they serve.

CONSEQUENCES

Consequences define what happens when rules are broken or followed. Because we are a punishment-oriented culture, consequences are often confused with punishments. A punishment is an action intended to make someone feel bad, to increase discomfort. The goal of a punishment is for the individual to learn from his pain to avoid doing the same thing again. Unfortunately, punishments rarely work. If they did, our prisons would not be overflowing with repeat offenders.

A consequence is designed to teach someone better behavior. The goal is for the individual to learn something from the experience so that she can make better choices. Just as a teacher has a set of instructional objectives and content designed to meet them, the classroom rules represent the instructional objectives; the consequences, the content that need be learned in order for those objectives to be met. Because children learn differently and at different paces, most teachers realize the need to have many ways of teaching the same material to ensure learning. Discipline works the same way. We cannot expect the same approach to work for all of the children when rules are broken. It is necessary to envision many possible consequences so that the teacher can always implement a consequence and still pay attention to individual needs. This is always desirable and quite possible when the class operates according to the principle, "I will be fair, and I will not always treat everyone the same." Too many teachers have felt compelled to use the same consequences in sequence for all kids, and the results are poor. That would be like expecting the Scott Foresman reading series to turn every single child on to reading or for all children to use the same batting stance to hit a ball.

It is with consequences that issues about "fairness" come into play more than in any other aspect of discipline. That is another reason why we teachers often decide to do it the same way with all kids. We want to avoid situations in which we feel forced into using a consequence that we know will not work with a given child just to maintain the integrity of the system. Ultimately, such systems fall apart. A better criterion regarding the use of consequences is to do what works.

We think of consequences as being of four types: (1) natural/logical, (2) conventional, (3) generic, and (4) instructional. A good discipline plan will blend the different types of consequences so that each rule has several consequences to teach better behavior. The teacher employs a consequence whenever a rule is broken. Here are examples of each type, but teachers are encouraged to create their own consequences that reflect individual teaching styles and classroom needs.

1. Natural/logical consequences. Natural/logical consequences bear a direct relationship to the rule. Wherever possible, these consequences are preferred. They grow naturally from the rule, so there is connection between the rule broken and what happens. In the "real world" outside of school, there are many examples of this type of consequence. When someone arrives late to the airport, the natural consequence is that she misses her flight. Coming home late for dinner may mean that the latecomer either eats a cold dinner or has to make his own. Going outside underdressed in the winter means that the individual will be cold. Teachers and parents often rescue children from the natural consequences of their choices. In my parent counseling groups, I often hear parents describe power struggles with their children over things such as meal times and appropriate dress. The parent nags her child to eat or dress right, and, when he does not, arguing ensues. After a battle of wills, it matters little who won, because usually the parent winds up exhausted and frustrated. It is better to "let the chips fall where they may" in order to teach kids good behavior. I have yet to hear about a child who has frozen to death while walking to school because she did not have on a heavy enough winter coat. Better for a child to experience the cold as a way of learning about appropriate dress.

In a school setting, natural/logical consequences can be used whenever possible. Some examples follow:

RULE: No throwing trash on floor
NATURAL CONSEQUENCES: Picking up trash
Cleaning the classroom

RULE: No talking when others are talking
LOGICAL CONSEQUENCE: Waiting five minutes before talking

RULE: Come to class on time
NATURAL CONSEQUENCE: Missing the instruction and still being responsible for it
LOGICAL CONSEQUENCE: Staying after class to make up for lost time

RULE: No name-calling "your mother"
LOGICAL CONSEQUENCE: Apologizing to the mother or telling her why you think that of her

RULE: We may not use or take anyone's belongings without her permission

LOGICAL CONSEQUENCE: Making restitution by giving the student something of yours

2. Conventional consequences. It is not always possible or desirable to use natural/logical consequences. For example, if an employee swears at her boss, she runs the risk of being fired. But students have tenure, and at most they can be suspended for a few days and then they are back. There are other times when implementing a natural consequence might be educationally unsound. For example, if a student refuses to read, the natural consequence of developing poor reading skills may have long-term negative effects. Conventional consequences represent things that many teachers have been doing for a long time that warrant being continued:

(a) Phone call home to alert parent(s) of problem

(b) Teacher-parent-student conference

(c) Referral to the principal for time-out

(d) Time-out in the classroom

(e) Earning privileges in class by acting responsibly (e.g., recess, play time at the end of the day, a pizza party)

(f) Calling the police if laws are broken

(g) Losing points or getting a zero (if achievement-oriented)

(h) Not earning classroom privileges

3. Generic consequences. These are consequences that can be used with any rule:

(a) Reminders: There are many variations of reminders that are effective when rules are broken. The most obvious reminders are (i) *verbal.* "Billy, we come to class on time here. This is your reminder." There are also (ii) *gestural* reminders in which the teacher works out nonverbal cues with individuals, small groups, or the whole class which signal the children that they need to improve their behavior. Some teachers have developed so many different signals for children that they look like third-base coaches passing along signs to a runner. A third type of reminder is a (iii) *written note.* I remember a junior high teacher who had 3 × 5 index cards with a different reminder or appreciation written on each one. Some cards said things such as, "Chill out, please . . . . Cool it . . . . Enough . . . . Danger ahead," while others said such things as, "Way to go . . . . Thanks for the cooperation . . . . Thumbs up." While teaching, he occasionally placed a card on the desk of a student. A few seconds later, he would come by and pick it up without breaking stride. Rarely did he have to do more to get improved behavior.

(b) Warnings: A warning is a stern reminder. It is delivered with an assertive tone that leaves little doubt in the mind of the student that a more active consequence is on the horizon. Like the warning label on a cigarette pack, it is intended to alert the user of the potentially damaging effects of the product. A warning is usually delivered in close proximity, with clear eye contact and a firm tone of voice. The message is, "What do you think will happen if this behavior continues?" There can also be self-warnings, as when the teacher says, "Sally, things are getting out of hand. I can give you a warning or you can give one to yourself."

(c) Choosing: We believe that it is sometimes best to give students a choice of consequences that they believe will help them improve their behavior. "Janelle, only one person may speak at a time. What do you think will best help you to remember that rule?" The teacher can provide structured choices but leaves the decision up to the child. "Max, coming to school prepared is necessary. Would a reminder, warning, or phone call home be best in doing that? Which one?"

(d) Planning: Developing an action plan for improved behavior is the most effective consequence for a wide range of rules. The best questions to ask to encourage an effective plan from the child are the following:

   (i) What have you done that is not appropriate?

  (ii) Why is it not an appropriate action?

 (iii) How is it harmful?

 (iv) What can you do to fix it and make it right? or, What is your plan for correcting that behavior?

4. Instructional consequences. These are consequences that teach children alternative behavior by providing opportunities for them to practice using their plans. For example, a child who is frequently out of his seat may need help:

(a) Distinguishing appropriate from inappropriate in-seat behavior

(b) Practicing appropriate behavior in the safety of the teacher's presence without the other students around; skills such as using I-messages, saying please and thank you, dealing with name-calling in nonviolent ways, learning to control one's anger, and thinking before acting can all be taught

When instructional consequences are implemented, the child usually stays after school or meets during recess or free periods to either learn or practice the skill. The books on "Skillstreaming" by Goldstein provide specific ideas about how to teach various social skills to children and adolescents.

QUESTIONS

1. Take a look at the rules that you developed for good learning and teaching (p. 69). Identify at least two consequences for every rule that fit into each of the four categories of consequences above.

2. Are there certain consequences you have used that do not fit any of these categories? Have they been effective? If they are dignified, help students develop an internal locus of control, and they work, keep them!

3. You may be able to expand your consequence options by seeking input from other teachers. You might ask for suggestions at a faculty meeting, or send around a rule to your fellow teachers and ask them to submit possible consequences that they think might be effective.

Since our earlier books, we have come to prefer unsequenced consequences because these give the teacher the greatest flexibility to do what is needed in a situation. Students know the possible consequences; and, if a rule is broken, the consequence most likely to teach the child better behavior is implemented. Once again, fair is not always equal. An exception is with populations of youth who have demonstrated the need for consistent structure because of limited cognitive skill or chronic social and/or legal problems. In those instances, a clearly defined set of rules and consistent consequences in sequenced order (first time, X happens; second time, Y happens, etc.) can be effective in providing the safety, security, and predictability they require. Some school discipline programs need sequenced consequences because there are different adults monitoring behavior with the same children at different times (e.g., cafeteria, halls, playground). It is important for all to be on the same page when monitoring schoolwide behavior.

GIVE A TEST FOR COMPREHENSION

One "Discipline with Dignity" practice that we have found highly effective is to give the class a test for comprehension of the rules and consequences. Since one of the most frequently heard reasons that students give for why they break rules is, "I didn't know," a test for comprehension eliminates that problem. The expectation is that each student must receive 100% to pass. The test may be oral or written and must have language that all children can understand. As motivation for passing the test, teachers are encouraged to connect it with earning classroom privileges. The test can be developed by the teacher, or students can submit questions (based upon their rules for the teacher and each other) as another way of increasing student ownership of the plan. A P.E. teacher from one of our courses at Seattle Pacific University recently shared a true-false test that she developed with her students: *

1. You are allowed to enter the gym any way you like.

2. You may wear any school clothes to gym.

3. Anything that is fun is permitted in gym.

4. When you enter the gym in silence, you remain silent until the directions have been given.

5. If you don't like what a classmate is doing, tell your classmates what a jerk you think he is.

6. We all have bad days, so being mean to classmates is understood and accepted.

7. If you break a rule, you may have to come up with a written plan for your behavior.

---

* My thanks to the student who prepared this examination, and my regrets for having misplaced her name so that I cannot properly credit her for her work.

8. Because you have entered the gym quietly, you can sit anywhere you like.

9. As long as you do your best on a given day, you don't have to care what anyone else does.

10. Gym is so physical that it is okay to "accidentally" hit someone as long as you think you can get away with it.

11. If you break a rule, you may have to practice ways of following the rule, either after school or on your free time.

SITUATION

What do I do when students use foul language in the classroom? That really bugs me. I'm from the "old school," where you never even considered using any four-letter word that starts with f, s, or sh.

ANALYSIS / SOLUTION

Gary Fahey, a Seattle teacher, explains how he solved a similar problem using rules and consequences:

> *I know that I can't swim upstream against this tide of swearing, but I have found that respectfully confronting students can make a positive difference. As I am a "Discipline with Dignity" advocate, I have established specific rules and consequences. Generic consequences such as reminders, warnings, and plans have been especially effective. In particular, saying things privately has really made a difference because it really is a way to get my point across while protecting the dignity of the student. With regard to swearing and use of foul language, I have found that having two additional consequences has helped to reduce this problem:*
>
> > *1. "If I hear you use that language again, I will assume that you do not wish to cooperate with*

that particular rule or in the proceedings of this class, so you will need to go to in-school suspension for the remainder of class and do your work there."

2. *"If I hear you use that language again, I may notify your parents (or guardians). Even though you may be permitted to use that language in front of them, it cannot be tolerated in the classroom. I will invite them in to join us in developing a plan so that you can use foul language at home but not at school."*

My area of teaching is secondary math, but my eyes have been opened to the need to really work with the whole student. We have developed social contracts, I regularly seek feedback from students to tell me what is working and what is not, and I continue to use positives like field trips, room environment improvements, special projects, and math brainteasers to keep up motivation. But most important, I have undergone a fundamental change in my attitude. I am committed to the idea that, when students come into class, they understand that they don't just bring that portion of their brain that absorbs math, they bring in all their humanity.

SITUATION

As an assistant principal at a middle school, I am constantly swamped with kids being sent to the office. Some teachers send kids for chewing gum or wearing hats, while others send for serious infractions. In "Discipline with Dignity," what should the role of the A.P. be? When do you advise teachers to send kids to the office, and when do you expect them to handle things within the classroom?

ANALYSIS / SOLUTION

Each classroom teacher is responsible for providing a set of principles and rules within the classroom. Principles provide the reasons for rules and/or the values that underlie each rule. For example, "Treat others as you want them to treat you" and "Show respect" are really values. They show how people should interact with each other. But they are not rules because they lack clarity and specificity. They provide the foundation for rules. Rules that connect to "Show respect" may include such things as, "Keep hands and feet to yourself," "Only one person may speak at a time," and "No fighting; if you are angry, you can tell how you feel, write your angry thoughts on a piece of paper, or wait until after class to discuss it with the teacher or student." They are clear and specific, and people can plainly tell whether or not the behavior has occurred. Rules and principles are best developed in a collaborative manner involving all the students. If rules are to be developed on a schoolwide basis, then representatives from all of the school community should be involved. Examples of schoolwide programs and the processes by which they are developed appear in Chapter 8.

Since most of the action in schools happens in the classroom, the teacher is expected to establish the discipline. Each is expected to have principles, rules, and consequences. When rules are broken, a consequence is implemented. In classrooms in which rules have been collaboratively developed, students take more responsibility for reminding each other when problems occur.

Administrators should serve two primary functions in supporting teachers and students. First, they should be available to deal with seriously disruptive behaviors that interfere with the teaching-learning process. Violence toward others or toward property, as well as verbal attacks, are examples. Second, when a teacher refers a student to the office for "minor" infractions, that teacher is feeling extremely frustrated and angry with the student. From her perspective, the choice is between sending the kid to the office or opening up the window and pushing him out. Administrators must recognize this level of frustration and support that teacher by not sending the student back to class until a time when the teacher and student may be able to work out their differences or agree to a truce.

The bottom-line consequence within a "Discipline with Dignity" format is what we call the "insubordination rule." Within the context of a caring, nurturing, empowering environment, there are still limits. If and when students chronically violate rules or refuse to accept consequences, it is our belief that teachers should not teach these students in the regular classroom until one or both occur. Teachers are still expected to provide instruction to the student but not within the classroom. Administrative support of the insubordination rule can make a major difference in your school. Use of in-school suspension or reliance upon collegial support, in which a student spends instructional time in a colleague's class, are two ways of providing such instruction. Administrators can also support their teachers by agreeing to teach their classes while they attempt to resolve problems with difficult students.

When administrators feel confident that teachers are doing most of the discipline, and when teachers know that they will be supported during (ideally infrequent) referrals to the office, disciplinary support and cooperation often improve.

A major administrative role is to be visible and present throughout the school. Too often, administrators are locked in their offices, dealing with the lines of kids who are sent there for discipline. When teachers do more of the discipline, this can free up the administrators to be present in "high discipline activity" places such as the halls, bathrooms, cafeteria, playground, and bus. Assistant principals can move beyond the "assembly-line" discipline mentality. Just as we advocate that teachers have a range of consequences designed to teach children better behavior, the administrator also needs a range of choices to move beyond the "warning-detention-suspension" triangle. An administrator's consequences should be congruent with those of the classroom teachers and should be instructional rather than punitive.

I recall working with a group of assistant principals in a state that has legalized corporal punishment. I asked them if it was effective in stopping misbehavior. There was a near unanimous "No." I asked them why they continued to do something that was ineffective. They said, "To show staff that I'm tough on student misbehavior." I issued a challenge. I suggested that, when students are referred and they are considering corporal punishment, they offer the students a choice. They can either take their customary "licks" or develop an action plan that specifically says how they will stay out of trouble. When I returned a few months later, I asked these administrators what had happened. They reported that the vast majority of students chose corporal punishment over planning. From the students' point of view, "licks" were easier than real change through thought. Instructional consequences can be "tough"!

Administrators need to be at the head of the movement from punishment to communication by establishing a caring, secure tone within the building.

SITUATION

My school has a policy against hats being worn at school. Believe it or not, this has become a divisive issue among staff, with some very supportive of the rule while others are not. More than an occasional hassle occurs with students about this. What do you think?

ANALYSIS / SOLUTION

The principle "Rules must make sense," is at the foundation of this question. There may be times when this rule is sensible, such as when it enhances learning and reduces conflict. There are some situations in which a hat may represent the colors of a gang. Hats may become targets for easy disruption by grabbing, tossing, or hiding. In these instances, the rule makes sense because the safety of people and property should supercede the freedom to choose one's clothing. Some might argue that a hat does not cause disruption, people do. Although far less serious, that thinking is analogous to "Guns don't kill— people do." While certainly true, easy availability makes use much more likely.

When hats are not disruptive to the learning process, there should not be a rule. Some schools have this rule because not wearing a hat is a sign of respect. I find that a much harder sell to kids these days, especially when many of their heroes such as Michael Jordan and Latoya Jackson are seen in many different settings wearing hats. In summary: when behavior has a concrete, tangible, negative impact upon instruction, there needs to be a rule; at other times, there is no need.

Some teachers might feel that hats interfere with instruction, while others do not. Having no school rule about this does not preclude individual teachers from establishing a "no hats" guideline in their classes. It is appropriate for a teacher to say, "When you have a hat on, I feel as if you are about to get up and go. That makes me feel rushed as a teacher. I would appreciate you helping me be a better teacher by taking off your hats in class. Thanks."

If hat rules have been established, in a class or school-wide, all staff must support and enforce them. When they do not, kids get the message that they can break any rule with which they disagree. If you disagree, work to change the policy. If, after consequence enforcements, a few children continue to break the rules, I have found paradoxically accepting messages (see Chapter 6) such as the following to be especially effective:

1. "Ken, you are an important member of our class with or without your hat. I guess I'll need to work harder to help you see that."

2. "Jim, I know how important it is at your age to feel noticed, important, and special. So I guess when you keep breaking the hat rule it must be your way of telling us that being noticed is more important than following a rule. I'll try to be more understanding."

3. "Bill, that's a great hat! If I asked you to take it off, you'd probably refuse. I'll keep working at convincing you that you are a very successful person with or without your hat."

SITUATION

I have found that kids who have trouble with their behavior are especially difficult to handle during the holiday season. Other teachers at my school have noticed this as well. We also go on heightened alert during the week before vacation because of the increase in fighting among students. It's tough because we (staff) get frazzled between trying to teach, deal with student behavior, and get our own holiday needs met. Any suggestions?

ANALYSIS / SOLUTION

Our society sells us a bill of goods, particularly during the holidays, that everyone is supposed to be jovial, happy, caring, loving, etc. There are thousands of commercials that portray people buying gifts for their loved ones or decorating the tree at home amidst loving parents and extended family. It is a very different picture from the one many children actually face in their daily lives. And if anything, feelings become more intensified during this time. A child who is struggling with depression is likely to become more depressed. One who has trouble with anger is more likely to have those buttons pressed. Stressed kids strongly feel the contrast between how their lives actually are with the images of how life ought to be.

A 16-year-old youth recently shared his distress at learning of his father's affair with the mother of his best friend. Worse, the father had been using the youngster as a counselor in an apparent effort to win the boy's approval. The boy was able to suppress for months the deep hurt and anger that he was feeling. But, when the holiday season rolled around and he and his parents (who were still together) were decorating the Christmas tree amid constant bickering between the parents, he exploded and shouted obscenities. His father demanded that he stop. One thing led to another and ended with the boy and his father having a fist fight, followed by the young man's leaving home to stay with a friend. The boy's depression and rage were also unleashed at school with cut classes, missed assignments, and a short temper.

During the stressful holiday season, it is especially important that teachers do a lot of active listening so that students will not feel alone. It is also helpful to give students opportunities to share and support one another. Give your students sentence stems and invite them to complete them either by writing or speaking. For example, you could ask kids to finish the sentence, "The best thing about the holiday season is . . . " Then, "The thing I hate most about the holidays is . . . " If the kids are unaccustomed to personal disclosure, then you can collect each of the sentences and read them anonymously, which will often lead to considerable discussion. One child wrote, "I hate that my mama is too poor and we can't buy a tree." The teacher discussed how hard it is to be poor during the holidays, when everybody is thinking about the wonderful things that he should get. She then invited this class of third-graders to imagine how that person feels. Words such as ashamed and embarrassed were used. This led to a discussion in which many children said that they would still want to be friends with the kid. It mattered more to them whether someone was nice or mean than whether someone was rich or poor. Some teachers have encouraged their students to become Santas to each other: "We can't all control how the holiday is for everyone outside of the class, but we can make an extra special effort during the holiday season to be special givers to each other. Let's think of all the things and ways that we can give to each other to make us feel good about being in this class and in this school."

At a school level, there is a heightened need for vigilance on the part of the staff during the holidays. Because of the increase in fighting and other discipline problems, it is especially necessary that staff be visible and present throughout the school to provide reassurance and a sense of safety. Administrators should avoid scheduling nonessential meetings throughout the week or two leading to the holidays so that they are available for teachers and students.

During the holidays, expect that the emotions of kids will peak. Provide opportunities for youngsters to share their feelings and offer your own. Share some of your own times of disappointment associated with the holidays. Let kids know that you understand how they feel. Remind students of the classroom rules and brainstorm with them some ways that the class together can remind and support one another if and when rules are broken. Finally, the holidays are an emotional time for teachers as well. You will need extra energy to cope with the increased emotional needs of your students. Understanding why they are acting out will allow you to be more tolerant.

Remember that holidays are times for giving, and the best gift they might receive is the care and understanding that you express to them.

5

Dealing with Power Struggles

PREVENTION is the most effective form of discipline. We have found over and over that those teachers who attend to the basic needs that drive behavior, and build their classrooms in need-satisfying ways, have fewer discipline problems throughout the year. Even in the best of circumstances, there are children who test the limits, are uncooperative and unmoved, despite your best efforts. In most instances, when rules are broken, the best way of responding is with privacy, eye contact, and proximity (P.E.P.). If the teacher is close, quiet, and direct, most children will readily accept a consequence. When a child will not, however, I have found de-escalation the best way of dealing with this.

While there are no ready-made steps or exact sequences by which to measure your response, a sequence similar to the following may help you frame a reasonably comfortable way of dealing with these moments. Most of us can become easily unnerved and quickly angered when children challenge our authority in front of the class. The "What are you going to do about it?" moments can be tense and uncertain. We all need short-term effective and dignified things to say and do when a student becomes challenging or simply refuses to accept a reasonable consequence.

Let us assume that Luis is a student in Mrs. Hernandez's class. He has been talking when others are talking and has been "playfully" slapping Henry in the head, disrupting Henry's learning and Mrs. Hernandez's teaching, as well as distracting others. Mrs. Hernandez has reminded and warned to no avail. She decides that "planning" might be an effective consequence and delivers this consequence with P.E.P. She tells Luis, "I'll see you after school today so that we can work together on a plan to stop hitting and to raise your hand when you want to be recognized."

Luis says loudly so that many in the class hear, "I can't come today after school. I'm busy."

The above scenario represents the first moves in a no-win power struggle. Most teachers, when faced with a student's defiance, either escalate the stakes or withdraw. Neither of these options is either dignified or effective. Let us see why.

If Mrs. Hernandez says, "You're staying. You should have thought about that before you broke the rules for the fifth time today," Luis has two choices. (1) He can back down and yield, and feel resentful in the process. This choice probably will make him look for another opportunity to attack, perhaps more sneakily. (2) He can decide to further the challenge by whispering under his breath or by brazenly continuing with a "Try and make me" frontal assault. If the challenge continues, it will escalate rapidly and result in a visit to the principal's office. Neither side has won because, unless it is June, there is always later today, tomorrow, or next week when that student will be back.

A wiser way of dealing with these moments is to realize that differences of opinion will almost never get resolved while the whole class watches. Mrs. Hernandez is best advised to minimize the disruption and, if need be, offer Luis an opportunity to present his side of things during a private time. We will now look at some better options for Mrs. Hernandez.

STEP 1

Luis says, "I'm not staying. I'm busy today after school."

Mrs. Hernandez ignores the remark and continues teaching. Julie asks her what she is going to do about Luis in front of the class. "That's a private matter involving Luis and me," says Mrs. Hernandez. She reminds the class that she never discusses one student with others. She continues to teach.

Approximately 60% to 70% of all possible power struggles will end at this point because you have preserved Luis's dignity. In many instances, ignoring these "hooks" works well because what the student really wants is to save face among his peers and has every intention of staying. After school, Luis shows up.

STEP 2

When Step 1 is ineffective, as it sometimes will be, Mrs. Hernandez goes to "active listening."

"Mrs. Hernandez," Luis repeats boldly, "I said I'm not staying. My father said I don't have to and I'm not going to."

Mrs. H. actively listens aloud. "Let's see, Luis. You are telling me you are not staying and that your father would approve. Did I get that right?"

"Yeah," Luis replies.

"Thanks for letting me know," Mrs. H. says politely. She resumes teaching.

A remaining 25% to 30% of all students will stop after active listening. They feel that they have been heard, they have not been challenged in front of their peers, and there is little reason to continue. But occasionally there is a child who will.

STEP 3

Luis pushes the issue, wanting to create a scene.

Luis, angrily: "I said I'm not staying and there ain't nothing you can do about it. Are you deaf? You can't do nothing!"

Mrs. H.: "Wow, Luis, you are really upset about this. In no uncertain terms you are telling me you are not staying and there's nothing I can do about it." She continues assertively and compassionately. "You may be right, Luis. There may be nothing I can do about it. I would like to hear your side of things right after class." She resumes teaching.

STEP 4

In the event that Luis keeps it up, Mrs. H. can acknowledge that a power struggle is occurring and invite Luis to make his case at a private time.

"Luis," she tells him, "we're getting into a fight about this. The time to continue this is after class, when I can really pay attention to what you are saying."

STEP 5

Should Luis continue, then it is time for him to leave for the day (sending to the principal or to a colleague for time-out). If that option does not exist, Mrs. H. can give more classroom control to Luis, especially if everyone has already been sufficiently disrupted through these events.

Mrs. H.: "Luis, you either need to stop, tell me after class, or leave if you feel you can't control it until later." In the event that leaving is not an option, Mrs. H. can walk toward Luis and quietly offer him the chalk and control of the class (a risky option, to be used only when control is clearly no longer possible at that moment). If he takes it, then she should sit in his seat and join the class as a "peer." Most students do not want the chalk and will stop right then.

STEP 6

Insubordination clause: We believe that any student who refuses to accept a consequence within a "Discipline with Dignity" classroom should not be permitted to remain in that class. He may return when he has accepted the consequence or has come up with an alternative way to demonstrate more responsible behavior. The teacher is still expected to provide assignments and indirect instruction, but not in class. The students know that this is part of the way the classroom works before there are problems. In most cases, Mrs. Hernandez is able to end the power struggle early because she and the class know that the insubordination clause is the bottom line.

When administrators support removal from class for this reason, or when teachers have arranged with colleagues to have each other's students in their class, that student's absence from class the following day is a more powerful statement to the class than threats or words. Invariably, there is at least one student (usually Luis, Jr.) who, the next day, smiling, asks, "Where's Luis?" That question provides the teacher with a wonderful opportunity to protect Luis's dignity and her own by saying, "That's a private matter between Luis and me. Today's lesson is . . ."

STEP 7

Assuming that Luis stopped escalating early in the sequence, Mrs. Hernandez can seek him out after class and remind him to come after school or acknowledge that, if that would be a hardship, together they may seek another alternative. She might say, "Luis, the real issue for me is for you to keep your hands to yourself and to raise your hand before you call out. If after school isn't a good time for you to develop a plan, when is a better time?"

STEP 8

Assuming that Luis had to leave the class because he kept escalating, Mrs. Hernandez should seek him out later to reconnect. She might say, "Wow, Luis, you and I really got into it today. You were mad and so was I. That happens sometimes. As soon as you have a plan, I'd love to see you back in class."

The steps to dealing effectively with power struggles are:

1. Ignore "hooks."

2. Actively listen to what the student is saying without agreeing or disagreeing.

3. Actively listen to the student's feelings without agreeing or disagreeing.

4. Tell the student that there is a power struggle developing and defer to a private time.

5. Remove the student from class or give more control.

6. Invoke the insubordination clause.

7. Remind the student of the consequences as the student leaves class if the power struggle ended between Steps 1 and 4.

8. Seek out the student later and try to resolve differences if you reached Steps 4–5.

To summarize, the best way of dealing with power struggles is to avoid them. Once you are in one, there are only two real options. You and the student can negotiate your way out ("Let's work out our differences in private"), or one side can refuse to escalate. Since the teacher is presumably the more mature of the two, it is he who needs to extend his hand of negotiation and/or refuse to escalate. To do so requires the ability to remain firm but anger-free. It presupposes that, when a student is hot and attacking, the teacher will be able to listen, care, and not personalize the assault.

To illustrate, I borrow a concept from the great family therapist Virginia Satir: "When someone is blaming or becoming angry, go into computer mode." We must be able to remain in control of who we are when another is losing or has lost control. Otherwise, we merely contribute to a chaotic situation. It requires skill and practice to learn how to go into computer mode when attacked.

Long ago, I was having trouble relating with a youth who always seemed to attack me verbally. Certain words made me want to go off on him. He knew how to press my buttons. Even though I knew his horrible background included abuse, I had trouble maintaining control in the face of his assaults. I went to a friend who noticed how upset I was. This was a man who was noted for having great discipline with all kids, no matter how tough they were. He told me that in his opinion I was giving away a great deal of power by reacting emotionally to the young man. My friend asked me how I'd feel if, instead of calling me an s.o.b., the kid called me a "typewriter" or a "plate" or a "can of Spam." I laughed, but at that time it was hard for me to see where this might have a place. A few days later, the kid loudly referred to me as the waste product that comes out of a horse's rear end. I found myself thinking, "Plate, Spam, typewriter... plate, Spam, typewriter . . . ." I began laughing. The kid probably thought that I had lost it. I remember looking him squarely in the eye and saying without sarcasm, "There's probably some truth to that. Thanks for letting me know." He stopped!

It is important that I remind myself of the times that I am responsible for the anger I get from others as a result of what I say or do: when I discount by not paying attention, when I am critical or blaming, when I expect unattainable performance, when the tone of my voice accuses another of being stupid, and when I come across as having the only right answers. In cases such as these, I can expect others to protect their dignity by fighting back.

When we feel put on the spot, we all need lines to say that are emotionally neutral and de-escalating. For practice, let us suppose that an angry child yells a put-down at you in front of the class. He calls you an s.o.b. or says, "You're unfair—always picking on me." Write down as many things as you can think of that would be emotionally neutral or de-escalating:

a.

b.

c.

d.

e.

f.

Let me share my list with you:

THINGS TO SAY WHEN CONFRONTED

(a) When did you start (feeling, thinking, believing) that? Tell me after class.

(b) Do you always (think, feel, believe) that way about me? When did it start? Let me know after class.

(c) That is an interesting opinion.

(d) I must not be showing up for you because, if I were, I don't think you'd say that to me. When we have some time, I'd like to know how I can improve and be a better teacher for you.

(e) I'm glad you trust me enough to tell me how you feel, and I'm concerned. Any suggestions for improvement are appreciated.

(f) There's probably a lot of truth to what you are saying. Sometimes you get angry when you think I've been unfair.

(g) When you call me names, I feel upset and kind of feel like attacking you back. But I know you are hurting inside, and I really need to understand about that if you are going to be successful in this class.

(h) You might be right.

SITUATION

How would an effective teacher defuse a pack of twelfth-grade, 250-lb. football players—playing off one another, jostling, talking, and constantly engaging in disruptive classroom activities?

ANALYSIS / SOLUTION

There are several possibilities. It is necessary to have specific rules that have been developed in collaboration with your students. You will need a variety of consequences designed to teach better behavior. The generic consequence of planning might work well. You could get together with each student individually or with them as a group and plan a solution to the problem. You could say, "You guys are too big for me to tackle. Most days, I feel like a quarterback on the football field with you guys chasing me. . . . If there is going to be learning in our class, I need you guys to join the plays. Maybe you can even call a few. Can I count on your cooperation? . . . How can I let you know when things are getting out of hand so that nobody gets embarrassed?" You could ask them for some suggestions about making the class itself more stimulating. The goal is to positively empower them by including them as problem solvers.

It may be appropriate to call one or more of their parents. Be sure that this is a consequence that all students know. Otherwise, a phone call home becomes a threat and punishment rather than a consequence. You could say, "The problem of messing around in class needs to stop because it is interfering with the learning of many students. Will you take care of it or would you prefer that I ask your parents to join us in solving the problem?"

It is necessary to show confidence and speak the language of the students so that they get the message without feeling attacked or losing their dignity. Students expect their teachers to be knowledgeable and interesting. When there is a lot of off-task behavior occurring, boredom is often at the root. It helps when the teacher invites her students to join her in exploring ways to make the class more interesting. Football players love action, movement, and hitting. A more "hands-on" approach to learning that includes physical movement may get them more interested.

Occasional feigned "temper tantrums" and the use of humor and nonsense are a few other ways to deal with the problem. Particularly with difficult-to-reach youth, there is a need for the teacher to balance a consistent, predictable approach with moments of unusual response.

SITUATION

What do you do with someone who absolutely refuses to do something? I asked a ninth-grade girl to move to another desk because she would not stop talking and she said, "No." After I repeated my request, she still refused. I said she had two choices— to move or report to the office. After she left, I felt there should have been something else I could have done. How could this have been handled differently?

ANALYSIS / SOLUTION

Sometimes sending to the office is an appropriate consequence when the child's presence becomes or remains too disruptive to the learning process. It is a judgment call that has no absolute criteria. It is best to use this consequence later rather than sooner because, when you send a student too quickly, you convey the message that you are unable to deal effectively with problems when they occur in the classroom. I would consider a sequence with this student such as the one that follows. Notice that many of the specifics are described in more detail on previous pages. Each strategy is used only if the one before is ineffective:

1. "When you (student's name) talk to your friend, it is extremely difficult for me to talk over the chatter. I'd appreciate your stopping. Thanks."

2. Using P.E.P. (privacy, eye contact, proximity), say firmly, "I asked you to stop talking, and I need that to happen now." Walk away as soon as you say this so that the girl can save face.

3. "I can see that socializing with your friend is more important than listening to me today. I have days like that myself sometimes. Thanks for reminding me that I can't always get everybody to do what I want."

4. "When you keep talking loudly, it serves as a reminder that we all need to do our best work even when there are distractions around us. That presents a challenge that I think we can meet."

5. "The talking is just making it impossible for us. You'll need to stop or go to the office."

This sequence provides the short-term "What do you say or do when . . . ?" kinds of solutions that are at best only part of the answer. No matter how things turn out in this situation, when you have a student who repeats the same behaviors that break the rules, then you must search for the basic needs that she seeks to fulfill through the behavior. Later, I would seek to meet with this student individually and acknowledge the obvious importance to her of socializing with her classmates. I would let her know that socializing is very important and that sometimes it is indeed even more important than paying attention in class. I would then attempt to jointly solve the problem with her so that we could find ways for her to socialize without interfering with classroom instruction. You might offer to be more understanding of her socializing while working out a private signal that you could give her if it really gets in the way of your teaching.

MEDIATING POWER STRUGGLES BETWEEN STUDENTS

During the course of a 180-day or longer school year, there are likely to be disagreements, disputes, and interpersonal problems that arise between students. Many such disputes respond well to mediation. Children as young as fourth grade have been trained to be school mediators. Many teachers can become mediators in helping students resolve their disputes. When problems arise, the students involved have the option of meeting with a mediator, who helps them find a solution. Mediators need to have good listening skills and know how to get people talking to each other rather than at each other. Look at a process we developed several years ago for disputes between teachers and students that has been easily adapted for peer mediation.

In this process, the mediator is called a "Coach." It is the Coach's job to keep communication flowing between the aggrieved parties and help them find a workable solution. The steps are as follows:

1. Coach introduces himself to both students.

2. Coach asks each student to take his turn describing what the other did that he resented, disliked, or made him feel angry.

3. Coach asks each student to repeat to the other what was said to ensure understanding.

4. Coach asks both students to say what they like about each other or what they think other people like about that person.

5. Coach asks each student to repeat to the other what was said to ensure understanding.

6. Coach asks each student to say what he wants the other to do differently that will solve the problem.

7. Each student repeats the other person's demands.

8. Coach asks each student who will do each of the desired things.

9. Each student repeats what he is willing to do, as well as listening to what the other person is willing to do, and an agreement is reached.

10. Students shake hands, put the agreement in writing (optional), and agree on a follow-up date within a week to make sure that the agreement is working.

The following example illustrates these steps in resolving a fight between two students.

Coach: Both of you wanted to get together because of the fight yesterday. My job is to help you guys figure out what else you can do to not fight and not get into trouble. Now, Pat, tell Laval what he did or what he does that bugs you. Laval, I just want you to listen for now. You'll get your chance soon.

Pat: He called my mother a name on the playground and took my books.

Coach: Tell Laval. Talk to him.

Pat: I don't like you calling my mother names and messing with my books.

Coach: (to Laval) Just to make sure you understand, tell Pat what he just told you.

Laval: You don't like it when I call your mother names and take your books.

Coach: Okay. Now, you tell Pat what he does or did that bugged you.

Laval: You don't ever play with me, and you and a few other kids you are with keeping making fun of me. You make faces and sometimes pick on me.

Coach: (to Pat) What doesn't he like?

Pat: He doesn't like when I make faces and pick on him with my friends, even though I don't.

Laval: You do too.

Coach: You don't have to agree with everything you hear just so long as you each listen. And you are both doing a good job of that. Now, Pat, tell Laval what he does that you like or what you think others like about him.

Pat: You share your lunch sometimes, and your Nintendo with other kids, but never with me. I like it when you don't cut in front of me in line.

Coach: (to Laval) What does he like?

(Laval repeats back.)

Coach: Now, Laval, tell Pat what you or others like about him.

Laval: I think you are smart and good at baseball. The other kids always want to be friends with you.

Coach: (to Pat) What does he like?

(Pat repeats back.)

Coach: Okay, now, you each know what you don't like and what you do. What are each of you willing to do so that there won't be any more fighting?

Pat: Well, I make faces at you because you never share your Nintendo or invite me to play. So I'd like you to play Nintendo with me, and then I won't make faces or get my friends to bug you.

Laval: I'd like to play ball with you even though I'm not very good. I'd like you and your friends to eat lunch with me sometimes.

Pat: Okay, how about three times a week you can eat lunch with us and I'll pick you next time we play ball to be on my team?

Laval: Well, if you want to play Nintendo, you can either play it with me at school or come over to my house after.

Coach: So what is each of you guys agreeing to do?

(Pat and Laval repeat the agreement.)

Coach: Sounds like a good agreement. *(He summarizes.)* Let's meet together next week to make sure that the agreement is working.

(Pat and Laval shake hands.)

One mediation session is sometimes sufficient to facilitate an agreement. Some disputes seem as intractable as the Arab-Israeli conflict and require multiple meetings. When there are many areas of conflict, it is fine to accept small agreements. Developing a mutual plan that works may mean that each small success provides motivation for the next.

SITUATION

What can I do about this violence in kids? It is really getting to me. I teach second grade and have been physically struck by a few kids on more than one occasion. One kid actually accused me of hitting him. But what is even worse is that the boy's father got involved and told my principal that he wanted his son to "beat the hell out of anybody who is trying to beat the hell out of him." While this father was especially frightening, it is commonplace for kids to tell me that their mother, father, or both tell them to solve their problems by hitting. While I'm trying to teach, their parents are telling them that fighting is okay. I am exasperated and just don't know how to go about handling this.

ANALYSIS / SOLUTION

Fighting cannot and must not be tolerated at school. We must establish the school as a safety zone. Learning, curiosity, and achievement cannot thrive when students fear for their safety. We live in a culture that glorifies, if not encourages, violent solutions to problems. That makes our job more difficult. Despite all of this, there are many things you can do to address this problem.

Some children claim that their parents tell them to fight back because it is an answer that often leaves us speechless. It is used as a good excuse. It is often sufficient to tell the child that unless the fighting stops, you will be calling home to arrange a conference so that you and the child's parent can discuss this issue. If violence persists, meet with the parent and approach the issue respectfully but directly. Tell the parent, "José tells me that his mom says that if anybody hits him, he is to hit them back immediately, even if this happens in school. Is José understanding you correctly?" Quite often, the parent will either deny or clarify that this is what was meant. This can lead to a good discussion of what messages the parent is trying to convey to the child and then some ways of doing it more clearly.

If the child's parent(s) support or encourage fighting, you will need to come to a meeting of the minds with them. Your best bet is to approach the issue in a clear, nonjudgmental tone. Acknowledge with the parent that sometimes fighting in life may be necessary, but that in school it cannot be tolerated because it interferes with children getting an adequate education. You can say, "I understand that you want Jamal to stand up for himself so that bullies don't pick on him. But Jamal needs to understand that school is a place for learning. For learning to happen, all children, including Jamal, need to feel safe. Jamal is a capable child who can really be successful in school with the right kind of help. He needs us to work together. I'm trying to teach the children how to solve their problems with their brains rather than their fists. Can I count on your help?" Proceed to explain some alternatives to violence that you are teaching.

You may need to "teach" the parent. In some instances, teachers have been successful making the analogy between school and the workplace. You might explain, "The goal of getting a good education is to get a good job. I'll bet that you'd like to see that some day for Jamal. Now tell me, what do you think would happen if you or another adult punched the boss or a co-worker because you became angry with him at work? Before you answer, just suppose that the boss or co-worker had been mean and said nasty things before you punched him. What do you think would happen?" Most parents can see that they would probably lose their jobs even if they had been provoked to anger by someone else. You can conclude with, "I see this classroom as Jamal's workplace, and he needs to learn better ways to handle himself when others make him angry."

In a few cases, it is clear that you will not be successful in influencing the parent. You may not even be able to get in contact with the child's parent or caregiver. In these instances, you should clearly communicate your expectations to the student. You can say, "That must be confusing. Your mama tells you to fight, and I tell you that you can't. I'm sure your mama has her reasons, and there may be some good ones for fighting outside of school." (You might offer some of these possible reasons so that the student senses understanding from you.) "But in school we do not fight. Instead we solve our problems by telling how we feel, by writing down our angry thoughts, and even by going to the 'chill' corner to cool down when we need to. Which of these solutions would you like to use the next time you feel angry?"

One of the goals of "Discipline with Dignity" is the "prevention" of discipline problems. Children who fight or otherwise misbehave frequently are often lacking adequate social skills. They need alternatives and opportunities to practice new skills and receive feedback about how they are doing with their new behavior. They need patience and an understanding that behavior changes slowly. They need to learn peacemaking and nonviolent conflict resolution. They can benefit from seeing their teacher frustrated or angry and watching as she finds a nonviolent, dignified way of resolving her issues. We believe that when you want to take a behavior away from someone, you must consider an alternative to put in its place. Be sure to have rules that tell children what they can do as well as what they cannot. Demonstrate, model, and explain what rules look like and sound like when they are broken or followed.

My colleague, Jim Fay, noted educator, author, and former principal, advises that when the problem is violence and involves more than one person, the aggressors should be confronted with the following assignment:

(a) Why do you think there is a "No Fighting" rule in the school?

(b) Do you think we should keep it?

(c) Why don't you see teachers or principals slugging kids in school? (Be careful about asking this one if your school endorses corporal punishment.)

The student aggressors are expected to jointly discuss and answer these questions. As one might predict, this process often cools down the parties, helps them see their behavior in a broader context, and gets them to work together cooperatively to solve a problem.

Finally, problems such as fighting can often be successfully resolved by involving the class as decision makers. We have found the following sequence to be a very effective way of accomplishing this:

1. *Identify the problem.* "Sometimes fighting goes on in the school. I'll bet that one reason why kids fight is because other kids call you names, or worse, they call your mama names. Has anyone ever heard someone say, 'Your mama (your mutha)'?"

2. *Get 'em thinking.* "Why do you think someone would call you or your mama a name? What reaction are they trying to get?

   (It is common for children or teenagers to most often mention anger and getting them in trouble.)

3. *Does it work? Is it worth the hassle?* Explore with your students whether fighting usually puts an end to the problem or usually just keeps problems going. Even if it does "work," is the person who called your mama a name worth getting into trouble over?

4. *Explore alternatives.* "Let's think of all the things we can say or do other than hit when someone tries to get us to fight." Write these down. Encourage the students to be as specific as possible. You can offer your ideas here as well. We have found that kids need to know and practice different "lines" that they can say when they are provoked. Some neutral ones that they usually will not think of but that you can offer are:

   (a) "You must have the wrong mama."

   (b) "You really make me mad, and I'd like to rearrange your face. But you ain't worth getting into trouble for."

   (c) "That's an interesting opinion."

(d) "I'm sorry you feel that way about my mama. I'll bet your mama is nice."

(e) "You're just trying to make me mad, probably because you're unhappy. I hope you feel better. Let me know if I can help."

5. *Seek good solutions.* Have students, either in small groups or as a class, evaluate each of the solutions to decide which are most likely to solve the problem. Post all of the "good" solutions in a place for everyone to see.

6. *Each student makes a plan.* Challenge all students to come up with a plan that has at least three things each one will do before either fighting back verbally or physically. Some students may need more structure from you, and you can list several "good" solutions from which they each pick three. They should each share their plan with you.

Unconventional Methods of Discipline

"Then, in spite of everything, I still believe people are good at heart."

— Anne Frank

O NE OF THE BASIC PRECEPTS of "Discipline with Dignity" is to stop doing ineffective things. As noted earlier, there are some students who simply do not respond to methods, interventions, and interactions that "work" with most. Whether due to biological, social, psychological, familial, academic, cultural, or intellectual factors, there are clearly some students who do not respond to most conventional methods of discipline. These students are often discouraged by the school process, with little hope that school achievement is within reach. They do not see how achievement will provide a better life.

One thing is clear: business as usual means more failure for the student and more aggravation for the teacher. Some of the methods noted in this chapter are intended to provide special ways of responding to "hooks" that lead to endless power struggles. Others are preventive in nature, in that they seek to prevent the continuation of such problems and help students begin to see school as more meaningful and need-satisfying.

Difficult youth need a lot of emotional and intellectual energy from us. Most of all, they need us to accept them even though they put up as many barriers as possible. They often make themselves unlikable, irritating, frustrating, and frightening. It takes enormous effort to deter these hostile behaviors and still have enough left to reach out to these needy kids. There is no substitute for keeping yourself healthy physically and emotionally. Pay attention to the basics of good health—nutrition, rest, exercise—and use whatever stress-control methods work for you: fun time with family, hobbies, friends, spiritual activities, mind and body relaxation.

Teaching difficult students requires that we change or suspend some fundamental beliefs while working with them. We need to let go of the need for such students to get better in order for us to feel worthy as educators. We need to remind ourselves that some kids feel forced into coming to school. It is natural for some not to thrive in a situation that is forced upon them. It is especially urgent that we address the basic needs of these students, because these provide the fuel for their problem behaviors. We must work at finding ways to accept the existence of difficult students without emotionally insisting that they mirror our expectations. We need to ask ourselves, "Can I focus on controlling my attitude so that the student becomes more important than what he does?"

Some of the ideas that follow can be easily transferred into specific strategies and techniques, while others require a shift in attitude. Both are necessary when working with difficult-to-reach students.

1. MENTORING

> *"I want to give back what I received. . . . I don't preach to anyone. If I see someone leaning toward where I was, I tell them how I got help. I listen to them. You got to be there to help. You got to do it. You can't assume someone else will be there to do it if you aren't."*

—Jonathan Savage
recovering alcohol and cocaine abuser
(as reported in the Rochester *Times-Union,* April 26, 1991)

It is my experience that the focus on single-parent *versus* two-parent families and their effects on child development has been overdone. There are too many kids from single-parent families who grow up without the social-emotional problems popularly characterized in the literature. Every child needs at least *one* important other who thinks she is the cat's meow—a person whose love is unconditional, who has high expectations, who believes in the child, and who *wants* to play and interact with, and to teach, that child.

Not only do single parents want good things for their children, they are usually active in providing ongoing messages about the importance of school achievement and success. These children are much more likely to be socially and academically successful than children who do not have at least one caring individual in their lives. Caring involvement and personal contact is much more important than intellectual aptitude and peer influence in defining success.

In the last few years, there has been an increasing emphasis on providing non-family mentoring for children at risk. Such programs as "I Have a Dream" offer hope to youngsters by dangling the carrot of a tuition-paid college experience in return for high school graduation. They also provide ongoing support during the school years to help children reach their long-term goals. Kids at risk often have very little long-term hope. Talk with an impoverished sixth-grader about the importance of school achievement and working his way out of the ghetto generally falls on deaf ears. Most kids are unable to look beyond today, tomorrow, or at most next week. Programs that offer long-term hope without the ongoing means to support a youngster's efforts are generally ineffective.

Mentoring programs that make a difference come in many shapes and sizes. They do share, however, common characteristics to accomplish their objectives. First, they all pair a "child at risk" with one or more "role models" who are supportive and caring without being "preachy." They offer training, structure, and advice to the mentor, who is taking on a rewarding and difficult job. Especially challenging is working with older students who have had years of hurt and disappointment. Trust is not something easily gained even when people genuinely care. Most students need a combination of social-emotional support and academic tutoring to encourage hope. Relationships that form between mentor and student often extend to arenas of life outside. It is not uncommon for mentors to take their students home, to their place of employment, to seminars, or out to dinner. Community-based partnerships of parents, business, church, and social agencies can work collaboratively with the school to define the needs of their kids and set up mentoring programs to address those needs.

There are mentoring programs that can be exclusively school-based and involve only school personnel. Everybody from the superintendent of schools to an entry-level custodian is welcome to participate. Identification of those students at school who need something more than the system normally offers is followed by a discussion of the needs that drive problem behavior. These are the "If only I had more time and fewer students" kids who either get lost in the system or who create disruption for themselves and others. Next, each student is assigned to a volunteer staff person whose job becomes that of "mentoring" that student. Staff training in communication skills may be offered, but the primary requisites of a successful mentor are a compassionate heart, ability to see life from another person's perspective, and a high tolerance for frustration.

The mentors seek out their students for short periods of time daily. Differences in attitude and achievement soon become apparent. It is up to each of the staff to determine how time will be spent. Some of the more popular choices are visiting the student at his locker for social interaction, offering to tutor, personalizing conversation with that student for a few minutes each day, periodically phoning the student at home to discuss problems or academic needs, going out to a school-sponsored athletic event together. The mentor commits himself to working with the student so that she may eventually develop academic, social, and/or financial goals. He supports the student while they work through the plan to achieve those goals.

I have found encouraging results in working with difficult secondary students through a program that identifies students and assigns each to a willing staff member who commits to making personalized contact with that student for at least two minutes a day for 10 consecutive days (adapted here from a suggestion by Dr. Raymond Wlodkowski, friend and author of *Eager to Learn* [1990]). Some of the communication strategies listed above are adaptable with this time frame. Many teachers in schools who have used this type of technique have reported positive change among students involved in the program.

2. ENCOURAGE THE POSITIVE

Behavior modification literature is loaded with examples of how improved behavioral change is accomplished through positive reinforcement. The goal of such programs is to "shape" better behavior by reinforcing (rewarding) small improvements in behavior. For example, a student who swears 50 times a day might initially be reinforced for only 40 swears, with the long-term goal being zero. With most children, extrinsic rewards can have an unanticipated but very negative impact upon motivation. There are many studies that have shown how rewards can increase angry competition among students, reduce creativity, and harm intrinsic motivation. Behavior modification programs may block the development of responsibility, because others are always making the decisions.

Behavior modification techniques have a place with intractable problems of long duration. They are appropriate when a student's choices may have long-term negative effects of which the student is either unaware or developmentally incapable of assessing. Students who are not interested in reading may suffer long-term negative effects by not reading. Students who cannot sit in their seats for longer than 10 seconds and who push, shove, or agitate others are likely to experience social rejection and isolation. Children who have chronically broken rules or have been in trouble repeatedly with school or legal authorities may need a well-controlled program in which even basic privileges are earned. When safety is the issue, using rewards for compliant behavior is sensible as well. The goal of all such programs is the transfer of control from others to control within.

Change will often occur through finding ways of approving and noticing the child when his behavior is acceptable. I am reminded of the principal of a middle school who walks around his school armed with a cordless telephone attached to his belt. From a distance, he looks armed and dangerous, but up close he is the sweetest, most caring guy I have ever known. This principal seeks "victims" to catch being good so that he can encourage them to continue their positive ways. He may call a student aside and retreat to a semi-private, out-of-earshot location where he proceeds to let the child know how well he did keeping out of trouble in the cafeteria by following the rules. He often calls the parent right then to share the good news. Before parting, he offers the student a way to save face. Many "tough" kids do not want their buddies thinking that the principal has called home with good news. They have a reputation to preserve. The principal tells the student that, if he wants to tell his friends that he is in trouble, the principal will back him up.

This principal uses privacy, eye contact, and proximity to give positive messages of appreciation. One reason why many difficult students get worse after being reinforced, rewarded, or affirmed by an "authority" figure is that they believe they have to preserve their peer reputation as being "bad." P.E.P. makes it possible to give such kids the attention and affection they really need in such a way that they can non-defensively accept it without losing face.

Within the classroom, teachers are limited only by their imaginations in finding ways to applaud and genuinely appreciate their students' efforts. Some ideas are notes to the student at school, a note sent home addressed to the student, a positive phone call home to the parent, a surprise treat. One of the best ways of encouraging ongoing parent support is to set aside time to call parents with good news when it occurs. That sets a positive foundation in which parents are more likely to participate in a supportive way when the student requires home-school cooperation around changing negative behavior.

3. CHANGE THE LABEL

I recall a situation a few years ago in which an eight-year-old who had been extremely disruptive was referred to a small, low-student-teacher ratio class for "emotionally handicapped" children. After the first few days of the expected "honeymoon," Joe's characteristic behaviors appeared—pushing, arguing, refusing to comply, out of his seat, pushing things off his desk, knocking over chairs. Mrs. Willis, his teacher, who was noted for her success in working with the most troubled children, took him aside and asked why he was behaving in such a manner. Joe looked her in the eye and said, "Because I'm emotionally handicapped." Joe had taken his label and decided to live in accordance with it. Mrs. Willis, undeterred, respectfully replied, "Joe, in this class, everyone is called emotionally handicapped, so that is no excuse here. There are rules to follow, and this is what they are ...."

Too often, children live either up or down to the expectations that they have learned from others. The "Pygmalion Effect" lives on. Not long ago, I was interviewing a nine-year-old who had been referred to me due to his short attention span, distractibility, and disruptive behavior. During the interview, I asked him why he thought he had so much difficulty settling down in class. He said, without a pause, "Because I have attention deficit hyperactivity disorder." While there is no doubt that children with such difficulties have a naturally tougher time adapting to the rigors of most school situations, they need hope in order to believe that they can improve their situation.

Changing requires educators to reframe a child's problem so that the child can be worked with in positive rather than punitive ways. In Brendtro's *Reclaiming Youth at Risk,* it is shown that when we change the way we label a child, many new options appear. For example, children who are discipline problems are often described in terms such as defiant, rebellious, nasty, uncaring, and insensitive. If we attribute a child's difficult behavior to "defiance of our authority," it follows that we will become angry and intolerant of the defiance.

It is human nature to either fight or flee when we perceive ourselves under attack. By contrast, Brendtro recasts such youths as having "defiant" behavior because they feel discouraged or dejected, like a failure, or hurt. When I look beyond the difficult behavior to the feelings of the child, my compassion and desire to reach out return. A "discouraged" child elicits a very different reaction in me than does a "rebellious" child. In fact, many angry, defiant children really feel discouraged and are depressed. If we want students to improve their behavior, we must recognize and address the discouragement.

I worked with Paul, an eternally late student who banged into chairs "accidentally" and who rarely came to class on time or prepared; failure to do homework was a regular problem. After much frustration, lecturing, and unsuccessful attempts at positive reinforcement, I felt angry and annoyed and began emotionally withdrawing from him. The more I withdrew, the stronger his "anti-authority" behavior became. I finally relabeled Paul as a discouraged learner who believed that the only way to get attention in class was to keep doing what was familiar to him. When I recast Paul in this way, I noticed that my feelings began to soften toward him. I was now ready to deal with things more effectively.

The ice was broken one day when I asked him to remain after class. We had had several one-sided lecture "talks" before. This time, I told Paul that I was very upset and angry when he did things to disturb my teaching and interrupt the learning of his peers. "But what is really most upsetting, Paul," I said next, "is that most students who do the things you do in this class really feel like failures. Because they have been hurt before, they believe that the only real choice they have is to keep feeling like a failure and disrupting. In case that is true about you, Paul, I will try to be more understanding when you disturb the class. But I also know that in this class there are a bunch of other ways for you to be successful without disturbing." I went on to list these ways and concluded with, "Of course, the choice is yours." That was the beginning of a remarkable behavior transformation in that class.

Wherever and whenever possible, we must stop labeling children! Only labeling that truly identifies what a person needs is productive.

QUESTIONS

Are there students whom you think of as rebellious or defiant? Picture one or more in your mind. What feelings are generated in you as you see this student? . . . Now think of the same student(s) and re-label that student as being discouraged or emotionally upset. Do your feelings toward the child change? . . . Can you begin to see or feel how you might react differently to the child's behavior?

4. SATIATION

This means doing something over and over until there is no longer any desire to do it. When we are hungry, we eat until we are full, or satiated. We have had enough. The same principle holds true with all behaviors. Children will keep doing things as long as there is some desire, hunger, or payoff. Children will keep hitting as long as they get what they want when they hit. If a child desires attention and learns that one surefire way to get it is to swear, provoke fights, or act stupid, then he will keep doing these things until there is no longer any need to satisfy. Satiation requires that the individual do something until he is so sick of it that the desire is gone.

A teacher decides that John's spitball throwing needs action. She has already talked with him several times, had him develop several plans for not throwing spitballs, asked him to clean up the classroom, and kept him after school. None of these things has eliminated John's spitball throwing. She decides that John shoots spitballs because he gains a lot of attention from his peers or maybe he has a fascination with putting paper wads in his mouth and cannot stop. She uses a satiation strategy. One day, she approaches John and asks him to stay after school to shoot spitballs. John looks at her with a devilish cat-that-ate-the-canary grin. After school, John is in his chair, and the teacher brings him a stack of paper. She tells him, without sarcasm, that in her mind throwing spitballs is a talent like all others. John can have the whole 40 minutes to shoot spitballs. The only requirement is that once he starts he is not allowed to stop until the whole 40-minute period ends. John begins with great gusto. The sound of the ripping paper, the taste of the paper, the thrill at watching the great distance of travel are heaven to him for about the first 10 minutes. Gradually, though, John's interest and desire wane. He sits back, wanting to stop, but the teacher holds firm to the agreement: you keep going once you start. After 40 minutes, John can't wait to leave. His fascination with spitballs is gone.

You can use this type of approach with all behaviors, and similar results can be expected. In the real world, it would *not* be appropriate for you to encourage the continuation of any behavior that might injure another person or destroy property. You would not tell Joe to keep banging on Lindsay, nor would you encourage Jane to keep writing on the walls.

QUESTIONS

Can you think of a student whose behavior is neither dangerous nor damaging but chronically disturbing to the teaching-learning process? Be specific in defining the behavior. Before using such a strategy, ask yourself which basic need(s) might be motivating the behavior? What classroom practices have you tried that address these needs? What other strategies might make sense? How might you use a satiation technique with that student (or class)?

5. BEHAVING PARADOXICALLY

A method related to satiation is paradoxical behavior. This technique is based upon a therapeutic approach by Victor Frankl that he called paradoxical intention. The use of this technique as originally described involves purposely instructing patients not to change. The basic underlying assumption of this approach is that people resist changing even when they wish to do so. Change is a difficult, slow process for all people. The insomniac resists sleep even when she wants to sleep. The person who fears heights, going outside, or riding in elevators resists change even when the desire for it is very strong. Virtually all such people know and understand that their fears are irrational, but knowing does not always change the behavior. It seems that phobic people, just like anti-authority students, resist change and help for fear of losing control. As long as they maintain their fear, they are able to keep their anxiety tolerable.

In using paradoxical behavior, instead of suggesting change, the person is instructed not to change. The insomniac is instructed to pay attention to not falling asleep. The elevator-phobic individual may be told to avoid elevators at all costs, to climb up a hundred flights of stairs if necessary, and to avoid even looking at elevators. In effect, the therapist is "siding" with the person's resistance. Instead of demanding change, the therapist encourages the behavior to continue and may even point out some of the positive, beneficial aspects of the behavior. After all, a person who will not ride elevators will never have to worry about getting stuck in one in a blackout.

When people are encouraged to continue exactly as they have been, external pressure is removed and, at a subconscious level, the individual feels freer to make choices, including whether or not to continue the problem behavior. When nobody demands change and when people find the person acceptable despite her problem behavior, change can be approached in a more relaxed manner. Change often occurs when there is less external pressure. A strong ability to accept people with difficult, problematic behavior and a sense of humor are two important variables in the use of the paradoxical approach.

Behaving paradoxically can be a very effective method with anti-authority students. The message from the teacher is a firm and acceptant, "I want you [student] to keep behaving exactly as you have been." To accomplish this with genuineness and without sarcasm, it helps for teachers to consider how the difficult child's problematic behavior is in fact of benefit either to the child, the teacher, or the whole class. Molnar and Lindquist (1989) describe this as "looking for positive behaviors." In effect, the challenge is for the teacher to identify positive motivations and benefits for the child's problem behavior.

The authors offer an example of a child who blurts out answers in class. Usually, the teacher would view this behavior as negative and perceive the child as out to get the teacher, embarrass her, show off, or control the lesson. When the view is negative, the teacher is likely to get into a power struggle with the child. Possible positive motives for the behavior might include: the student being eagerly interested in the subject matter, the student liking the teacher and wanting to help her out by making sure someone answers, or the student having a desire to help the teacher ask more questions during the course of the lesson. With these positive motivations in mind, the teacher can respond with language such as, "Kristen, thanks for helping me out. I was a little worried that nobody would answer and then I'd have to keep doing all of the talking. That is really considerate." The child's problem behavior has been appreciated, and it is now fully up to Kristen to decide about change. The teacher could also see the benefits of the problem behavior to Kristen's classmates. She might say, "Kristen, when you call out an answer without raising your hand, I bet that your classmates are happy because, in case you give the wrong answer, it spares them the embarrassment of being wrong. That's very considerate."

There are many habitual problem behaviors that can be changed with paradoxical responses. Let us take a look at some common problems with sample responses:

PROBLEM—Wandering around the classroom: "Sally, you have a lot of energy, and that is good. Some people really need to get that energy out by walking before they sit down and work."

PROBLEM—Class clown: "Fred, you are funny. Thanks for a break in the routine. Your jokes give me and your classmates a moment to stop and laugh. Thanks for thinking of us."

PROBLEM—Refusal to participate: "Karen, you obviously are a thinking person who needs to be sure that you have thought things out well before you put it down in writing. Thinking is a good thing. When I see it in writing, I'll know you've given it a lot of thought."

PROBLEM—No homework: "Jack, I'd prefer that you do homework, because I think that would give you good practice with your skills. But when you don't do it, that gives me more time to spend helping others learn. It is unusual for someone your age to be as thoughtful about your classmates. I'll bet they appreciate it."

PROBLEM—Tardiness: "Luisa, I'd prefer that you be in class right on time. But you are here for 35 out of the 40 minutes, which is nearly 90%. Keep up the good work."

Now it is your turn. Consider a student who frequently does something or things that you find very irritating. You have already tried many conventional methods to effect change with little or no success.

(a) Identify the student.

(b) Describe the problem behavior.

(c) Identify positive aspects and benefits of the student's behavior. How do you, the class, or the student benefit from the problem behavior?

(d) Imagine that the student is in front of you, and try to express these positive benefits in a genuine way.

(e) Once you feel reasonably comfortable, then you should communicate in this way when the problem behavior occurs. Do not expect to be fully comfortable at first because what you are doing will feel unnatural for a while.

You must be genuine and sincere in your comments. If you behave paradoxically but with sarcasm, only the sarcasm will be felt and the power struggle will continue.

6. ENCOURAGING AN ALTERNATIVE

Most people resist behavior change even when they know it is in their best interest to accommodate the change. Virtually all people who overeat and under-exercise "know" that they should change their habits. Most who smoke "know" that they are probably reducing their life expectancy. Even when we know specifically what to do differently to improve our health, many either do not do it, or try it and then return to the familiar. It is human nature for people to have a predictable, stable routine, and change is frequently resisted even when for the better.

People accommodate change more readily when they do not feel forced to let go of the familiar. I was able to quit smoking only after several marginally successful attempts (i.e., quitting for a week). It worked for me to keep seeing myself as a smoker because, each time I thought that I had licked the habit forever, the urge to smoke had returned. After I followed an Alcoholics Anonymous model day by day (actually hour by hour), in which I never said that I was finished smoking forever, the desire to smoke was so reduced that, eight years later, I feel *almost* able to say that I will never smoke again.

Children who chronically misbehave can be thought of as "addicted" to their misbehavior. Even though many want to "quit," the exciting, familiar behavior keeps them going. Wanting to stop is not enough even when the potential consequences of continuing are serious.

An illustration is Julio, a 14-year-old "juvenile delinquent" who had been incarcerated in a youth facility for several months. Julio was a bright, capable street kid, the kind of kid who made people think, "If only this kid channeled his potential into school—wow!" The night before he was to be released, I met with Julio in the mostly barren "room" in which he was practicing his "Three-Card Monte" skills. Julio guaranteed that he was finished with getting into trouble. He would never do crime again. His intentions were genuine; he never wanted to be locked up again. Two months later, he was back.

Promises, wishes, and desires are not enough when dealing with addictive behavior. Kids in trouble need to know that getting out of trouble is going to be tough and that changing their behavior is going to be difficult. They need help seeing alternative ways of doing things and the support to take the risk to behave in a manner different from the familiar.

In a school setting, kids need compassionate teachers who understand that change is difficult. When a student fights a lot, it is pointless to lecture or punish the behavior without providing an alternative and an understanding that using the alternative requires guts. It is beneficial for the teacher to acknowledge that the "inappropriate behavior" may in fact be necessary at certain times.

A street kid, who believes that "tough" is necessary for survival, needs us to acknowledge that fighting may in fact have a place but is not allowed or tolerated in a place of learning. Such a student can be told, "Henry, I'd like this school and class to be a safe place, different from the toughness needed on the street to survive. When someone calls your mama a name here, I'd like to think that there may be less violent ways to solve that problem. But we all need a reminder in the real world that a 'don't mess with me' attitude is sometimes necessary."

The goal is to teach behavior change by allowing a different behavior to grow alongside the familiar without insisting that the familiar disappear. Mrs. Lewis, a teacher and mother of a bright but school-disaffected eleventh-grader, recently sought advice on how to "motivate" her child. He usually did no homework and seemed content with C's and D's, along with an occasional F. When I asked her what she had already done, she went through the familiar litany of the caring parent—talking to him, eliciting promises, grounding, taking away privileges, promising desired rewards for better grades, yelling at him, and finally becoming exasperated. With what seems like intractable behavior, the behavior itself becomes the centerpiece of this mother-son relationship. Where once she had been fond, loving, and supportive, she was now primarily punishing, nagging, and annoying. Mrs. Lewis needed to re-learn how to affirm and support her child. The strategy was for her to understand that, for him, achieving well at school was difficult, unimportant, or threatening. She needed to realize that low achievement is not a fate worse than death (although many parents and educators have trouble seeing it that way) and that it takes years after high school for many young people to find their own talents and interests.

Since he had established a pattern of school non-productivity, changing would not be easy for him even if he wanted to. Knowing these things helped her reach out to her son. When she received his report card with poor grades, instead of repeating her pattern of negatives, she dealt with him in a supportive way. Her message was, "Lon, you know I'd prefer to see A's and B's, but what's really important is how you feel and what happens to you. I've been thinking that maybe you don't see yourself as able to achieve well. Maybe you figure that if you really tried hard you wouldn't do well anyway. Then you'd probably really feel lousy. In case any of this is true, trying to do well at school would require a lot of courage and risk. You know that I am on the side of working harder, but you are more important to me than your grades." Mrs. Lewis's changed attitude enabled her to begin loving her son again. It also put the responsibility for deciding where it belonged—on her son.

Encouraging alternatives supports the child and shows an understanding of what might be motivating her choices. When people do not feel forced into changing, they are more likely to consider another way.

QUESTIONS

Think of a child with whom you are frequently in conflict. List the objectionable behaviors. What are the benefits to the child of behaving in these ways (e.g., nobody will mess with me, I won't be laughed at, I won't have to worry about feeling stupid if I try hard and don't succeed, etc.)? . . . What would you like the child to do instead? Practice communicating what you want the child to do differently ("I would prefer"), and say that you know it takes courage or guts to do the unfamiliar.

7. SPECIAL COMMUNICATION STRATEGIES

Most difficult-to-reach students have been reprimanded, reminded, or talked to thousands of times every year. Many eventually become immune to the familiar blaming, scolding, nagging, and lecturing. More of the same is unlikely to succeed. Here are some alternatives that may work:

I-STATEMENTS

Using I-statements is especially important in communicating concerns and expectations with students. An I-statement expresses the concern of the sender by (i) describing the behavior of concern, (ii) sharing feelings, and (iii) giving a reason for the feeling and/or setting a limit. Listed are some examples of I-statements:

"When you come late to class, I feel annoyed and distracted because everyone looks up and stops paying attention to their work. I want you here on time."

"When put-downs are used, I am disappointed in the hurt done to each other. We can't learn when we worry about bad names being called."

"When fights occur, I am concerned about safety, and in this classroom we solve our differences peacefully without fists."

QUESTIONS

Think of behaviors you find objectionable. How can you let a student know without blaming or lecturing? Practice using I-statements in as many places and with as many people as you can (your spouse, live-in, child, merchant at the store).

NEGOTIATION OPENERS

Rather than getting locked into or continuing power struggles, try reaching out to students with the following words and attitude:

"This is going to be a rough day if we keep nagging at each other. I know you don't like it and neither do I, so how can we make the most of this time? Why don't you think about that, and so will I."

"Let's take a look and see what is and is not working for me, for you, and for both of us."

"I must not be showing up for you because if I were, you would not be doing this. What am I doing wrong? How can I improve?"

"Let's see if you can help me solve my problem." Present how the student's behavior interferes with your teaching in an I-statement format. "Any ideas? . . . What if you did _____ and I did _____? How do you think that would work out?"

QUESTIONS

Now try making your own statements. Can you see that when you take responsibility for contributing to the problem, there can be more of a spirit of joint problem solving than when only one side is expected to change? It does not matter who is really right or wrong. It matters that conflict gets resolved, that the class stops being disrupted, and that the student doing the disruption sees other possibilities within the class. Think about ways to communicate these things.

SUPPORTIVE STATEMENTS

Many students who misbehave repeatedly really feel that there is little hope for success in the classroom. Most have come to view themselves as intellectually or academically inadequate. Bad behavior becomes a mask for protecting against feeling stupid. Edward Hackett (1990) recommends that teachers support low-achieving children by telling them at least three times weekly that they understand school is very hard and their best efforts are appreciated.

8. PETS IN THE CLASSROOM

Pet therapy has been a benefit to elderly and sick people who live alone and in nursing homes. When people feel lonely, pets offer companionship and unconditional love. Children who have been hurt, abused, who feel disconnected and frightened are sometimes able to communicate with a pet much more effectively than with people. They provide a soothing, calming effect that is quite real. A pet often addresses "basic needs" and can make a person feel important and connected. When a person cares for the pet properly, he is empowered and develops feelings of competence. The pet helps reinforce feelings of virtue and generosity by seeking him out and cozying up. There are many moments of fun.

A pet in the classroom can even affect discipline. A sixth-grade class in an inner-city school had a brown-and-white pet boxer named Peaches. Due to a Health Department rule, the dog was removed. The children took it upon themselves to write to the Health Department, eventually enabling them to get their pet back. Among their written comments (as reported in the Rochester *Times-Union* of May 1, 1991) to health officials were:

"She is wonderful. When I feel sad I pet her on the back and then the happiness comes right back to me."

"If we can have hamsters, rabbits, and gerbils, why can't we have a dog? When Peaches is here, it seems like the day is better and the class is filled with joy."

"She doesn't care if you are mean, nice, or what color you are. She will come to you."

The principal said, "Students . . . would go over and pet the dog if they had a family problem or something was bothering them." The teacher added, "Peaches even helped keep the classroom quiet. When the noise level rose too high, she would whine and the children would quiet down. Peaches didn't like a lot of noise. She is truly a stabilizing force in the classroom."

9. CHALLENGE KIDS TO FIND THEIR DIGNITY

Many youngsters who act out frequently are living out the negative stereotypes that others attribute to them. I have seen many students mobilize more healthy, prosocial parts of themselves when they are challenged to act differently from these low expectations. Tell your students, "I wonder if you realize that there are people in this school who think you act like animals. They expect you to act like jerks because that's what they think you are. Every time you slug, name-call, or whatever, that just reminds them all over again that you don't really belong. Now, do you want to give them the satisfaction of thinking that? I know that you aren't a jerk, and I'll bet that you know that you aren't a jerk, so why would you want these people to think that you are? What do you think you [we] could do to begin changing the ways people think of us? I know that you can be successful, and this is how. . . . What do you think?"

Along with this type of communication, I believe that it is important to post rules that are okay to be broken in your class. These rules should comprise the stereotypical expectations that you believe affect the negative achievement and/or behavioral decisions students make. A sample list of such rules is as follows:

RULES WE ARE ALLOWED TO BREAK

1. I have to fight whenever someone calls my mama a name because I'm very worried that other kids will think of me as a wuss if I don't.

2. It's stupid to work hard because I'll never be smart anyway.

3. Inner-city kids are stupid and can't learn as well as other kids because they are poor.

4. Kids like us [inner-city, learning disabled, ED, BD, the Redbirds] can only fight or run away from things when work gets hard because we are too dumb to think.

5. Being a drug dealer is the only real way of being successful if you are poor.

QUESTIONS

What are some other negative stereotypes or expectations that you think kids who are unsuccessful believe? How can you express your knowledge of this in rules that kids are allowed to break? Discuss this with them. Have them explore their beliefs about these issues. Help them see that they have choices.

10. REFUSE TO REJECT THE CHILD

Rejection is a familiar companion for many children who have severe discipline problems, and they will often do things to invite that response. These kids have learned not to trust, often with good reason. To trust again and get close can be terrifying if there is deep fear of reawakening these feelings only to be rejected again. Because the kids are angry and feel reject-ed, they often reject before someone else has the chance. They thus avoid taking the risk of getting close to someone who might let them down again. They need to know that you under-stand how they operate *and* that you are not going to abandon them, even when they behave in inappropriate, unacceptable ways.

I recall Jackie, a fourth-grade child who was entirely out of control in her special-education classroom. She had been sex-ually assaulted by her father, who later left her and her brother. Her mother eventually lost custody of the children due to neglect. Placement in a series of foster homes, where she again was sexually and physically abused, followed. Jackie became so unmanageable that subsequent foster parents returned her to social service authorities. After a few weeks of "honeymoon," she began her assault on the classroom, with unprovoked aggression toward the teacher and students and refusals to fol-low rules and the routine. Her teacher became frustrated and had to work to manage the distress she experienced in working with this child.

Behavior modification programs were at best short-lived in facilitating behavior change. The teacher knew that the child needed love. She did not know how to love someone who rejected most of her efforts. Mrs. Campbell finally learned to become confrontational with her love. She began approaching Jackie with an understanding of Jackie's reality and ways of reacting to it. She said, "Jackie, there have been important peo-ple in your life who have really hurt you a lot. They have hit and hurt you in ways that make me want to cry. When you call peo-ple names and hit others, I know that that is your way of push-ing us away before we have a chance to hurt you. You are very special to me, and I will not hurt you even when you want to hurt me. You may not believe that, but I mean it. So whenever you say bad things or hit others, I'll know that you are feeling especially afraid and that you need to settle down. When you feel hurt or afraid, you can come talk to me right then or go to the 'calm down' chair until you feel better. I cannot let you hurt others even when you are hurting so much yourself."

Children who are themselves emotionally or behaviorally out of control are extremely stressful to work with. Remember that taking good emotional care of yourself, doing stress-reducing activities, refusing to take the child's anger personally, and having a support network of others will all help you to deal with that stress.

11. HIGHLIGHT THE FACT THAT THERE ARE ALWAYS CHOICES IN LIFE.

A few years ago, I was working with a group of disaffected, turned-off kids. They were getting into trouble at school, having skirmishes with the law, and experimenting with drugs and sex as young as 11 and 12 years old. I had been asked to work with this fringe group in hopes of helping them do better. Nobody knew quite what to do with them, and I guess they figured that sending them to the psychologist would be some kind of viable solution. Always eager for a challenge, I spent considerable time structuring my thinking and activities to get at the key issues affecting their decision making. For several weeks (we met once a week), I just could not seem to get through to them. I felt little connection with the kids, as I felt that their walls of defenses kept them from risking being who they were.

During this time, there was a bumper sticker that was gaining much popularity. It seemed that everywhere I drove I would see several cars with it. It said, "SH— HAPPENS." I was really annoyed at the implication of the saying, because, while unpleasant things happen whether you like it or not, it occurred to me that, when one lives a life according to this dictum, there is little control or ownership over how things turn out. I believe in the value of teaching responsibility through internal locus of control, and this saying was anathema to me. During a school vacation, I went to visit my colleague and dear friend Rick Curwin. He and I were catching up on what each of us was doing, and I mentioned my hatred of this bumper sticker. I told him that it was not so much the saying that I minded as it was the finality of it all. I told him that the bumper sticker should continue on with a more hopeful message. Rick said, "How about 'SH— HAPPENS, BUT YOU DON'T HAVE TO STEP IN IT'?" That was it! That was the handle that I needed.

I could not wait to get back to my group. The first day back, I brought in the "SH— HAPPENS" bumper sticker, hung it up in the front of the room, and observed as each kid walked in with a shocked look on his face. I asked how many had seen the saying. All hands went up. I asked them how many believed that life was this way, and I was astounded to see a bunch of resonating heads nodding up and down.

I then issued a challenge. I asked them to imagine that they were listening to their favorite radio station when the news came on. They were too tired to turn it off, and they impatiently waited for the music to return. The last person on the news was the weatherman, who issued a very unusual weather report. I told them that weather people usually say things such as, "It'll be partly sunny with scattered clouds or scattered showers with a high in the 80s." Well, this weatherman said, "The forecast tomorrow is for scattered sh— to happen sometime between 11:00 a.m. and 3:00 p.m. There is a 50% chance that it will happen. It may be heavy at times . . . ."

The kids were now totally in disbelief. I continued by asking them to consider what each would do if they heard the report and had to go out between 11:00 and 3:00 through the place where that weather was predicted. "What would you do," I asked, "to minimize being totally covered by the weather?" For the next several minutes, we brainstormed, and the kids were more animated than I had ever seen them. Among their responses: bring an umbrella, wear a raincoat, wear boots, wear thigh-high boots, bring along perfume, call ahead to make sure there is a shower at the other end, pack a change of clothes, wear an oxygen mask.

This lesson became a wonderful metaphor for the real "sh—" that was happening in the lives of these kids. They needed help seeing that while they could not always control the events around them, there were choices in the ways of dealing with these events and the feelings they triggered.

It is often difficult for kids to really understand that they have choices. We need to level with them. We should be actively discussing the contemporary problems faced by youngsters and exploring choices with them. For example, kids who fight back because they are "dissed" (disrespected) by others take a huge risk. As increasing numbers of kids are armed with weapons, winding up dead is a reality that today's student faces. Walking away may be life-saving! Seeing choices in behavior and in one's reactions can be very positively empowering.

12. THE TOUGH BOTTOM LINE

In his book *Inside the Criminal Mind,* Samenow (1984) presents an approach to behavior change with hardened adult criminals that I have found effective with the most "antisocial" children. He claims that there are really only three choices available to the criminal regarding his behavior and choices. These are:

(a) Continue doing what got you in trouble and probably end up nonstop in a place like this (prison).

(b)   Kill yourself. Aside from a few people who are attached to you, nobody is very likely to miss you, and the world will probably be a better place without your crime.

(c)   Change your ways, which will not be easy because you are a hardened criminal who doesn't give a damn about anyone but you. It may be hard, but it is possible. If you decide on (c), let me know, and we can begin doing some work.

I have adapted this approach to a few "incorrigible" students with long-term histories of anti-authority behavior as a way to break through the barriers they often erect. The modifications in regular schools and when working with youth are:

Choice (a): Keep doing what you are doing and probably wind up getting kicked out of school or maybe even locked up.

Choice (b): Quit school and do everybody here a favor by taking your disturbing behaviors elsewhere.

Choice (c): Consider change, which for sure will not be easy for you since you have thrived for so long doing things against the rules. If you decide on (c), let me know, and I will give you all my support.

SITUATION

How can I deal with students who have trouble concentrating? There are two children in my third-grade classroom who just cannot pay attention. They are not malicious, and they seem eager to improve. They make promises to do better, but something always happens that gets them off track. One child has problems at home; but the other has loving, well-adjusted parents and siblings. I have tried reminders, warnings, and rewards, all

with minimal success. Recently, another teacher had a student who was put on Ritalin, and she told me that it was like a miracle drug. The child was able to pay attention, and his achievement began to improve in the classroom. Should I talk with my children's parents about getting them some medication?

ANALYSIS / SOLUTION

You describe some of the characteristics associated with "attention deficit hyperactivity disorder." ADHD has been widely written about and studied without any definitive findings. ADHD is a syndrome characterized by problems with attention span, impulse control, and sometimes hyperactivity. According to the American Psychiatric Association's DSM III-R, there are 14 symptoms associated with the syndrome, and at least eight of the symptoms need to be displayed for six months or more before a diagnosis is made:

1. Fidgets, squirms, or seems restless
2. Has difficulty remaining seated
3. Is easily distracted
4. Has difficulty waiting his turn
5. Blurts out answers
6. Has difficulty following instructions
7. Has difficulty sustaining attention
8. Shifts from one uncompleted task to the next
9. Has difficulty playing quietly
10. Talks excessively
11. Interrupts others
12. Does not seem to listen
13. Often loses things necessary for tasks

14. Frequently engages in dangerous actions

The diagnosis of ADHD can be quite difficult, and even subjective, since many of these symptoms exist among normal children and adults at least occasionally. This is made more complex by the fact that there are some children who are not hyperactive but who have problems with distractibility and organization. They may even appear quiet and passive.

Rarely are children with this diagnosis found to have a specific neurological problem. The latest speculation is that there is a biochemical cause for ADHD in which one or more of the brain's neurotransmitters responsible for attention and concentration is either overactive or underactive.

Those children who frequently display the above symptoms risk school failure and low self-esteem. Medication is rarely effective as a sole treatment, although those children who show positive change to the medication usually do so quite quickly. A multiple approach to treatment, including behavior programming, proper educational intervention, medical management, and personal counseling is usually most effective. As a teacher, focus on the educational, behavioral, and counseling components.

Establishing the proper learning environment for ADHD children can be accomplished in a number of ways. As part of the regular class seating, many ADHD children perform best when seated near the teacher with few distractions. Stimuli such as traffic from the outdoors, the tapping of a fellow student's pencil, the hum of a heater or air conditioner, and the rattling of windows can be distracting to such students. They also tend to perform well when a schedule is predictable, with explanation and preparation during transition times.

Such students need contact with positive peer models. Arranging cooperative learning opportunities in which an

ADHD child works on a project with a group of high achievers can be quite productive. Teachers should be sure to make directions clear and concise. Maintain eye contact while giving verbal instructions. You may want to approach the child and ask him in private to repeat them to be certain that he understands. Many teachers have found it helpful to make sure that such students write down all assignments correctly before they leave class. ADHD children may have difficulty organizing and remembering. Having a home-school notebook signed by a parent on a daily basis can ensure monitoring and relevant teacher-parent daily communication. Finally, many ADHD children have difficulty with planning, developing goals, and sustaining efforts toward long-range projects. Some may benefit from a program of rewards, and most need help to become better at planning and figuring out when to reward themselves.

A program of "self-monitoring" can be quite beneficial in helping such students train their thoughts and behaviors in a more effective way because it reinforces an internal locus of control. In these programs, responsibility for monitoring and perhaps rewarding is turned over to the student. The student may be asked to "rate" her behavior and, in the early days of the program, must come within range of the teacher's rating. Over time, the responsibility is gradually shifted to the student until the student no longer needs any external reward either from another or to give to herself. Children with ADHD need to be reminded to stop and think before acting. Two approaches that we have found helpful in teaching "stop and think" strategies to ADHD and non-ADHD children with problems of impulse are Camp et al.'s "Think Aloud" (1977) and Meichenbaum's (1977) "Problem-Solving":

"Think Aloud." When encountering a problem, children are trained to ask themselves the following questions and provide an answer before asking the next question:

(a) What is my problem?

(b) What is my plan to solve the problem?

(c) Am I using my plan?

(d) How did I do?

"Problem-Solving." This approach includes the following elements:

(a) What am I supposed to do?

(b) I need to look at all possibilities.

(c) I have to focus in and concentrate.

(d) I have to make a choice.

(e) How well did I do?

Children with ADHD often have social problems due to their impulsivity. It can be very helpful for the teacher to collaborate with some high-status children to find ways of being more tolerant and understanding. Their cooperation can be gained by saying, "Phil gets picked on a lot in class. I know that he sometimes calls names, bumps into kids, and bugs you when you are playing a game. Phil cannot always control this and needs us to find ways of being his friend, especially when he is having a rough day. How can you be his friend?"

Students with ADHD tend to achieve better when learning is presented with an experiential (hands-on) component. They may also need to move about more frequently. Relaxation methods such as deep breathing and guided imagery may help children become more focused and attentive.

SITUATION

I am a preschool special education teacher, and I am seeing increasing numbers of kids who just can't be controlled by usual behavior management methods. For example, there is a

two-year-old girl who won't look anyone in the eye, refuses to remove her coat, and cries for hours each day. A three-year-old boy in my classroom routinely wrecks toys and clears off classroom tables. He refuses to allow anyone near him. It turns out that these kids are "snow babies" who are growing up. Their mothers were using cocaine or other harmful drugs during pregnancy. It seems that new methods of behavior control need to be found because the old stuff just doesn't work. What can I do about these behavior problems that are due to maternal drug use?

ANALYSIS / SOLUTION

You are right that children whose mothers used cocaine or other harmful substances during their pregnancies often have unique problems. Not all children are affected. There are four common characteristics shared by many such children. It is rare for any child to have all of these reactions. These are:

(a) *Hypersensitivity.* Many children are extremely sensitive to normal sensory experiences. A bright light, passing traffic, the whir of a fan can spark a tantrum or withdrawal. Even experiences that we often think of as nurturing, such as rocking, singing to them, or stroking them, can be upsetting.

(b) *Social distancing.* They often do not make friends easily and prefer to keep away from other children and adults. Many do not like to be held or touched.

(c) *Short attention span.* The average attention span for a three-year-old is between 10 and 20 minutes, assuming the provision of proper, developmentally appropriate activities. Drug-affected children can rarely tolerate more than a few minutes. Learning is dramatically affected by this deficit.

(d) *Little tolerance for frustration.* Many of these children become easily overstimulated, have short attention spans, and prefer to be left alone. They have little patience for complex activities and toys.

Patient and innovative care is required. Children who fit these criteria need a variety of resources. Many have orthopedic and neurological problems requiring physical, occupational, and speech therapies. A team approach is needed. You will probably need to tone down your classroom to accommodate such children. Muted lighting and sound, as well as having specific routines, can be helpful. Teaching and learning goals should be brief and readily attainable. Teachers who work with such children should be well trained in calming activities. Some children can benefit from massage, soft music, a lotion rub, or playing with a favored texture when they seem agitated. Many children do not respond consistently to the same stimulus. Soft, soothing music one day may increase agitation the next.

We have seen several drug-affected children make progress with this type of approach. Some have increased their language skills, while others have increased their tolerance to touch and have an improved ability to handle frustration. But a big question that remains is what these children will be like as they get older. It seems that most, if not all, of the more severely affected children will require specialized, individual programming.

SITUATION

What do I do on days when the kids are off the wall? Some days, my classroom is absolute chaos—one crisis after another. I'm so tired of always dealing with petty squabbles and serious interpersonal conflicts. Can you suggest some way that I can teach my students to deal with conflicts on their own so that I have more time to teach the things that I want and need to teach?

ANALYSIS / SOLUTION

There are many things that you can do, but you must first realize that when children lack the skills to solve their own problems, they must first learn the skills before they can use them. You will need to invest some time teaching strategies in order to prevent the continuation of these problems. We hear many teachers of younger children complain about the time they spend resolving silly disputes like cutting in line and sharpening pencils. Most children have been taught that, instead of fighting, pushing, or otherwise taking matters into their own hands, they are first to tell the teacher.

This leads some children to become helpless because they always look for someone else to solve their problems. Children need to learn the difference between what to tell you and what to deal with on their own. Teachers need to know if kids are doing something that might endanger themselves or others. By contrast, when less crucial things occur, the best strategies are those that encourage them to do their own problem solving. For example, when one child cuts in line in front of another, you could say, "Lucinda, I can see you are really upset by what Janet did and you are telling me rather than fighting. I'm glad about that. Now, can you tell me what you might do on your own if she does this again? What is your plan?"

If Lucinda has no plan, then give her some time to develop one. Say in a friendly, supportive tone, "It sounds as if you need some time to think about that. When you have a plan, I'd like you to let me know." Another example in teaching a child responsibility when nonserious matters occur: "Too bad it was your pencil that Carlos took. What a bummer! What are you going to do about it?"

In Brainard and Behr's *Soup Should Be Seen, Not Heard! The Kids' Etiquette Book,* skills for dealing with many common, everyday situations are provided for young children. Sample questions addressed are:

1. What is the key to being polite?

2. How do you know what to wear to a party?

3. When is it okay to spit?

We can no longer assume that many children have the social skills to deal effectively and appropriately with daily "common-sense" situations. That is why one of the leading principles of "Discipline with Dignity" is "long-term behavior change rather than quick fixes." Self-management and conflict-resolution strategies can be taught to children to help them better manage their own behaviors.

7

Working with Parents

ARENTS CAN BE PARTNERS in providing an effective program of discipline in the schools. Just as we need to know how best to relate to contemporary youth, our efforts must also be directed at reaching the many parents who are "at-risk" of dropping out of their kids' school lives. Let us first explore the leading issues in the lives of parents that make for tenuous parent-school partnerships.

Overwhelmed parents. Many families are struggling for survival. Their attention is focused on living day-to-day and making ends meet. The growing homeless population and those who live below poverty level suggest that too many parents and children must focus their energies on safety, security, and survival as priorities over reading, writing, and arithmetic. Without sensitivity to the pain and hopelessness felt by parents, there is no way to connect with them at school. At an abstract level, almost all parents want their children to succeed at school because they know that school success is a way out of hopelessness. Unfortunately, making that desire a priority and accessing the energy needed to support children's academic efforts takes a back seat to the more prominent issues of survival.

Academically unsuccessful parents. People who have previously been in the hospital often experience anxiety and fear when they visit a friend or otherwise approach hospital grounds. The sights, sounds, feel, and smell of the hospital trigger uncomfortable memories, and many feel a sense of relief when they leave. For some parents, the sight, smell, and sounds of a school trigger similar recollections. Those who were academically and/or socially unsuccessful may have left school but not the memories of the experience. They grow up, have children, send their children off to school, and then relive aspects of their own childhood through their children. Some prefer, perhaps even need, to avoid the discomfort.

Parents with inadequate parenting skills. It is increasingly common for parents to be more uncertain than the child's teacher about how to handle their kids. We are becoming a culture in which children are rearing children. Latchkey children often rely on themselves or on an older sibling for comfort. They may see little of their parent(s). The explosion of teenagers having babies means that those babies will be reared by children who lack the maturity to simultaneously handle both their own development and that of their child. When teachers call home to discuss a child's behavior, it has become all too common for the parent to throw her arms up in resignation and concur with the teacher that she too is having problems with her child. In other cases, parents defend their kids as a way to deny family problems. The parental message is: How can you expect me to deal with a problem as trivial as Billy not doing his homework or fighting in school when I'm faced with Billy's out-of-bounds behavior all day, not to mention my own problems? Deal with it yourself, teacher, because I need a break!

Personally preoccupied parents. Parents often feel forced to choose between staying home and parenting or furthering their own careers. We are culturally unsupportive of parents who wish to do both. Daycare programs at work, job sharing, and time off for child-rearing are still practices or concepts that occur infrequently and often without cultural approval. A parent who has worked eight or 10 hours a day is going to have difficulty coming home and "working" for another hour or two on his child's math homework—especially if dinner needs to be made, things need to be cleaned, and bills have to be paid.

Some parents have substance-abuse problems that create a different definition of "personal preoccupation" and are significantly deleterious to providing the personal nourishing that their children need.

School-underinvolved parents. There are many schools, perhaps most, that profess to be open and involve their parents and communities but that are in fact quite unwelcoming. We rarely encourage parents to sit in our classes, walk in the halls, participate on curriculum committees, or give us their feedback about our teaching. By middle school, it is rare that regular parent-teacher conferences are scheduled. In too many instances, it takes a classroom problem for parents to be contacted.

While most parents rate their schools as "good" or "better," it is a rare school that truly seeks parents as partners. Sadly, parental involvement is too often limited to the most persistent parents, those with a deep educational commitment, or those with a personal axe to grind. Better discipline occurs in classes where students are involved in key decisions about issues that will affect their lives, and this principle applies with parents.

They must feel welcome and like more than "window dressing" when real involvement at a school or classroom level is the goal.

SCHOOL PRACTICES THAT ENCOURAGE POSITIVE PARENT INVOLVEMENT

Make your classroom and school a welcoming place. If you are a parent, ask yourself about the characteristics of teachers whom you find most appealing. Teachers who inspire success in children lead my list. As a parent, I prefer teachers who listen more than they talk at parent-teacher conferences. I like knowing that they care about what I think, that my views about my child will be taken into account in the classroom.

Teachers who are welcoming may call home before the start of the school year to introduce themselves and ask parents about their child's preferences and prior learning experiences. One Rochester, New York, school has its teachers spend the first few days prior to the school opening visiting parents door-to-door in the community. Parents feel welcome when there is a place for them in the classroom.

Some teachers have found it effective to call each parent prior to the beginning of the year and offer a range of activities that will need parent support and sponsorship. Each parent can be asked to help in a preferred activity. Secondary teachers can randomly call 10 to 15 parents a week (two or three a day) and formally or informally discuss issues of relevance. All teachers should try to focus their first few parent contacts around positive issues. Many parents are more cooperative with those teachers whom they believe like their children and see both the good and the bad.

QUESTIONS

1. What practices does my school currently have to make school a welcome place for parents?

2. What school practices would turn me off if I were a parent at the receiving end?

3. What specifically do I do now to encourage positive parent involvement in my class?

4. What have I thought of doing, or would I like to do, that I have not done yet?

5. If you are a parent, who are your child's teachers that you most admire and respect?

Seek parent input for decision making. The Rochester, New York, model of school restructuring includes "school-based planning." All non-mandated school issues must first get the approval of the planning team before they become school practice. Many schools have increased their parent participation because each school is required to have significant parent representation on the team. Although it takes longer for decisions to be made, they are often more effectively implemented because they have a broad base of support. This collaborative, problem-solving communication model is being adopted by many school districts throughout the country.

Many school districts have adopted the parent-involvement Comer model, named for an eminent Yale University psychiatrist. The model seeks to increase parents' participation at their children's school. The program was initiated in an economically depressed school in New Haven, Connecticut, and has steadily grown. It involves reaching out to parents in the community so that the school becomes a welcoming place for them. The principal and teachers will often walk through the community, knocking on doors of their parents to describe what the school needs and how that parent can become involved. Although this is a time-consuming, sometimes frustrating process, the results at schools that have heavy, positive parent participation are very favorable. Conventional methods of reaching out for parents, such as telephone calls, open houses, and PTA meetings, are ineffective for many. It is necessary to first meet parents on their own turf to bring them into the school. This means going out into the community, knocking on doors, and welcoming parents to come to school to become involved in their child's classroom life. Many teachers are reluctant to go into the neighborhood because of the discomfort they might feel in encountering life outside their own personal comfort zone. It is quite different "knowing" that your school is in an economically depressed area and actually sitting in a squalid apartment infested with rodents. It is one thing to know that drugs are used in abundance, and another to walk past the drug gallery. Active parent participation at school needs to begin first with educators reaching out, even when it may be difficult or frightening. Parents who have met you are more likely to help avert or solve crises concerning their children. My experiences with many schools confirm the power of parent involvement in making a difference in all facets of school life, including a reduction in student discipline problems.

At a classroom level, teachers should invite parents to be partners in finding solutions to the problems that affect their children. There is rarely one right answer, and when Nina is having ongoing classroom problems, her parent(s) may be invited to brainstorm possible causes and solutions in a collaborative spirit with her teacher. Saying such things as, "I'm concerned that Nina isn't getting all that she can out of the class, and I'd like to put our heads together to see how things might be improved," is perceived differently from, "Nina is being disruptive in the class, and she won't be able to remain unless she improves." It is crucial for parents to know that you think they are important and that you value their input in order to elicit that spirit of cooperation.

Encourage parent visibility at school. It amazes me that, when I see parents walking in the hall, eating in the school cafeteria, using the school bathrooms, sitting on the school bus, participating in their children's classes, I see much better behavior from the children. Kids are more likely to access appropriate social skills when in the presence of family or community individuals who are at school. Parental presence sends kids the signal that community expectations are transferable to the school. Although parents run the risk of occasional indigestion in the cafeteria or a headache on the bus, their presence should be sought and appreciated.

Involve parents and grandparents as volunteers. Some schools never have enough money to provide the kinds of academic and social opportunities and interventions necessary to help children. Others do better when the economy brightens but are forced to cut back or eliminate needed services during the lean years. While this yo-yo is not likely to be stabilized, there are many schools that have wisely turned toward parents and grandparents for experiences, assistance, support, and remediation, which provide a wonderful buffer against political and economic uncertainty when integrated into the school. Getting family intimately involved with the school is not without its risks and stresses. It takes time to recruit, train, and coordinate parent volunteers. Some teachers may need to work to change their stereotypes of parents as nosy, judgmental adversaries. Parents may need help in putting away their own negative school experiences. Further, the realities of today's society include working parents and many single parents. Child care and release time from work are important factors that influence a parent's ability to become involved. Several studies have linked parent involvement to significant gains in student achievement and more positive attitudes toward school. Ways of involving parents need to be developed at each school, depending upon its needs. Grandparents are often more available and eager to help. The following involvement practices provide a guide to services that many schools can coordinate to make a positive difference:

1. *Assisting in the classroom.* Parents and grandparents may read to children, tutor, help prepare materials for the day's work, or coordinate an upcoming field trip. Each teacher might ask herself, "What do I not have enough time to do that I value and think is important?" The family may be able to provide some services related to those needs.

2. *Supervision around the school.* Many schools have discipline problems on the playground, in the halls, bathrooms, and cafeteria, or on the bus. Insufficient supervision is often a common factor in these problems. Parents can be visible on the playground and perhaps even create a recreation program. The presence of two or three parents near the school lockers during class changes or riding the bus may prevent fights and unruly behavior.

3. *Providing instruction.* All communities have talented people who may be interested in offering their talents to the school on a voluntary basis. A parent musician may be willing to offer private instrumental lessons. Another might organize a chorus. An exercise program can be offered at the school with community volunteers. After-school "latchkey" programs may be staffed by parents, grandparents, and interested community citizens. Parents can be "guest" teachers, while others might help staff a telephone or after-school homework helpline. Some might become part of an organized mentoring program to help children who need special attention.

Provide frequent and ongoing feedback. Parents need to be informed in a timely, meaningful way. It is my opinion that, except in cases where there is known or suspected abuse, phone calls home at the early stages of problems can be very effective at eliciting parent support and cooperation. Sometimes it is useful to establish systems of ongoing parent-teacher feedback through letters, a newsletter, or a daily report card that notes accomplishments and needed improvements. It also helps parents when you are authoritative to the extent of your capabilities. For example, when you have specific suggestions for improvement to make and you see how parents can support that improvement, you can offer parents a variation of the following: "Let me tell you what is going on . . . ." "I want to describe what I'm going to do that will improve things . . . ." "Let me describe how you can help me work with your son [daughter] . . . ."

Connect with community resources. My vision is for schools to be the community hub around which a variety of services and supports are provided. We have evolved from a culture in which family was the primary support for children to one in which there are too often no predictable and/or stable influences supporting the academic and personal development of the child. The school is the most logical place for the networking that so many children and families need. There are a great many hurting, unsupervised children, and the school needs to assume a function once filled by healthy families. The school should be the unifying "agency" that connects a variety of support services needed by the child and his nuclear family. Communities no longer provide this type of support either. Nowadays, 45% of all people in our country do not even know who lives next door.

Schools with a vision need to tackle the provision of on-site daycare services for latchkey kids. Schools need a babysitting service so that parents can come to school and be "visible." Church leaders need to be welcome in our schools so that kids see the connections between the people and experiences in their lives. Businesses need to be encouraged to continue and further refine their adopt-a-school programs. They need to know that it is in their best interests to provide release time for parents to be involved in their children's school lives. Parenting-skills programs should be offered in school for teenage parents. One psychologist and social worker of my acquaintance has established a clinic at a school site for parents, children, and families that provides various counseling options for the family of any student in the school program. Schools should provide alcohol- and drug-abuse interventions and support systems at school for parents.

Providing these kinds of services has become an urgent need. All kids come to school, and school is the logical place to provide more than academic learning. Naturally, many resources and dollars are needed to make this happen. Perhaps the day will come when our political leaders will take their heads out of the sand and invest in our future. Schools that provide strong leadership by having much of the community involved can begin to make important differences in the lives of their children. The more that school becomes a personally meaningful and relevant place by incorporating its community's life realities, the better it will become at increasing the positive participation of that community.

8

Schoolwide Discipline

THE PRINCIPAL is the most important source of inspiration, support, and leadership needed to facilitate change within the school. Because effective schoolwide discipline requires that people of differing perceptions and roles work collaboratively, it is the principal who must set an effective tone for this work. Leadership requires an active principal whose presence is felt and who sets the tone by having clear, consistent rules.

A leader is unafraid of accountability to staff and students and demands the same from them, respectfully and with dignity. A leader is visible in the halls and cafeteria and at the bus stop. He smiles, greets his staff, knows the names of his students, and, most important, garners community and parent support by reaching out in ways such as making home visits. A leader is able to see the larger picture and coordinate community resources such as business and church, law-enforcement and private agencies, in order to maximize all possible input to the school.

These days, schoolwide discipline often requires a coordinated effort for any real change to occur. The drug problem, for example, is beyond the scope of the school alone to solve. Business leaders, volunteering as mentors, need to inspire hope in schoolkids that there can be a successful future without drugs. Those children who are already on drugs need the resources of rehabilitators to find alternatives to a chemical high. Church leaders may help fill spiritual voids, while law enforcement may provide the resources with which to guarantee a safe school environment. Parents can organize "hall watch" teams that offer more ongoing adult supervision and visibility in high-traffic corridors. An energetic principal organizes such resources and increases the potential impact of each other's efforts.

Schoolwide discipline provides challenges not seen at a classroom level, although the basic problem-solving process (see Chapter 4) is the same. All schools need a set of guiding principles that define what the school stands for. Mission statements and school philosophies often provide such principles. In addition, there needs to be agreement on policies concerning behavior in certain school-community places such as the cafeteria, hallway, playground, and bus. Although individual teachers will not always agree on the importance of certain rules, it is necessary that they support the rules of the school in a similar manner.

For example, even if an individual teacher does not see the need to take off hats at school, but school policy includes that rule, we believe that all teachers need to support it. This suggests the need for a more uniform system of enforcement for school rules than exists in the classroom. Naturally, all staff who are opposed to a rule should work within the system to change it. But, until it is changed, it is important that the rule be enforced. Otherwise, students learn to follow rules only in the presence of some adults and not others. This places unfair pressure on those who enforce them. Worse, kids learn that the only rules that are important to follow are those with which you agree. Because "Be a model of what you expect" is a guiding principle of "Discipline with Dignity," we must align our behavior in accordance with what we expect of kids.

The best schoolwide discipline plans are those that reflect the sentiment of the community. When there is a problem to be solved or a desire to reconsider current policy, a representative cross-section of the school community, including parents, teachers, students, administrators, and perhaps outside agencies (depending on the problem), are most likely to develop a plan that has a broad base of support. Although this process will often take longer, the solutions are more lasting. The following process will likely be useful when schoolwide problems occur or policies are reconsidered.

Define a focus for the problem(s) to be solved. What are the prevailing issues of concern to the school community? There may be few or many. Behavior on the playground, in the cafeteria, in the halls, in the lavatory, on the bus, and walking to school are the school-community areas in which it seems that nobody and everybody is in charge. Perhaps there are students wandering the halls during class or there are fights that generate concerns for personal safety. What is each teacher's responsibility for schoolwide discipline? At some point, concerns will be raised by some of the school community about one or more of these issues.

To more accurately define the problem, all relevant personnel should share perceptions and clarify how people see the school as it is and how people want the school to be. Faculty meetings, PTA meetings, the student council, joint meetings with community leaders, and questionnaires are ways of gaining this information. Some people may have considerable reluctance to share their views, particularly those who silently disagree with what they imagine to be the prevailing opinion of those in positions of authority. It is essential that a spirit of openness be fostered through nonjudgmental listening during this process.

Good leadership is especially important here. It can be helpful for perceptions and concerns to be shared anonymously. Each staff, student, or community member can, for example, be instructed to write down on a slip of paper "a problem at school that you would like to see improved to make the school a better place" and "one obstacle that you believe gets in the way of solving schoolwide problems." The meeting facilitator (probably the principal) collects each of the papers and reads the answers aloud so that all are apprised of each other's perceptions.

Prioritize the problems to be solved. It is now necessary to assess which of the problems will be given maximum attention. These may include cafeteria misbehavior, bathroom vandalizing, student smoking, or hall problems. Role groups may brainstorm which of these problems is of greatest concern. A committee or committees may be formed to more extensively study the problem(s) and generate preliminary solutions.

Generate possible solutions. The job of a committee is to study the various complexities of any problem and consider these when formulating possible solutions. When the constitution of the committee reflects a cross-section of the school community, the chances are much better that all of the nuances which may be obstacles to solutions will be explored. The committee(s) can develop preliminary solutions to the problem(s).

Present possible solutions. Feedback mechanisms need to be established so that the information can be shared with everyone. These mechanisms can include sharing at faculty meetings, PTA meetings, in the classrooms with kids, with the student council, or through sending packets of work in progress to important others. All should be encouraged to offer verbal and/or written feedback within a specified time frame.

Assess the proposed solutions. "Discipline with Dignity" requires that all discipline strategies meet at least three standards (and ideally, those on p. 55 as well):

1. Will it work long term as well as solve the short-term problem?

2. Will it teach students to be responsible (internal locus of control)?

3. Does it dignify or humiliate? (Put yourself on the receiving end to answer this.)

It is also important that the solution be congruent with the school's philosophy, guiding principles, and local and state regulations. I recall a high school that wanted to solve its "tardy to class" problem. The solution receiving greatest support was, "Lock your doors after the late bell rings." The halls would then be "swept" by administrators, with students receiving either warning, detention, or suspension depending upon how often they were late. When examined against a backdrop of the above criteria, it became clear that only those who were occasionally late and still largely motivated to achieve in class would care enough to get there to avoid being locked out. Others would have even more reason not to attend class. What does locking doors teach students about their own responsibility when it is the teacher who is doing the locking? Finally, how would teachers feel if they were late to class and found their rooms locked by the students? While such a procedure could have been nixed for any of the above reasons, it turned out that locking doors presented a fire hazard and was against state regulations.

Agree on solutions. After discussion and debate, proposed solutions are voted upon, with those receiving the broadest consensus being implemented.

The process and result of solving a schoolwide discipline problem using concepts of "Discipline with Dignity" is illustrated by the following model* from an inner-city elementary school:

The biggest and most noticeable feature of Valley View school is children. Their presence is everywhere. During the school day there is no place in the school without them. They move about, clearly demonstrating their belief that Valley View school is theirs. After school, the children's presence is immediately felt, even when there are no children present. The school atmosphere is warm, supportive, creative, and energetic. Yet discipline problems were a real part of the school, and we were asked to help the school devise and implement a program that would resolve these problems without destroying the openness of the school.

Our first step was to talk with a representative group of teachers who met regularly as the Instructional Council. This group reflected the various subject areas and age groups of the school. They identified an inconsistency throughout the school between the philosophy of the principal and the teachers and the actual methods used by administration and teachers. The more we talked, the more the gap seemed to widen. Further, we heard teach-

---

*Reprinted from Richard L. Curwin and Allen N. Mendler's *The Discipline Book* (1980).

166

ers say that openness is fine, but there was a significant population of students who abused the system and rendered it dysfunctional.

We needed to know at this point whether or not this inconsistency was a major incompatibility of ideas and/or behaviors, or rather a communication dysfunction. After careful data collection, we discovered that although there was a wide range of philosophical interpretations, teachers shared a similar view of the basic goals of the school. Further, the problems as perceived by the staff were remarkably similar. But the staff never had open discussions about the goals and purpose of their school. Thus, differences were imagined. And these differences were intensified by individual teaching styles and the need for communication.

Once the staff was confronted with the data we collected, things began to happen. First, there was a need for greater communication among themselves and with the administration. In fact, they were willing to work during the summer without pay to establish a viable communication program. Second, they were able to identify specific problems in the school that were sore spots for them. By dealing directly with these problems, they could relate better with everyone. They could allow their differences to co-exist and the similarities to provide a unity and consistency that was previously lacking.

We decided to deal with the immediate problems first. In a total staff meeting, we brainstormed all the school problems that the teachers could not solve individually. These were the overall problems that the openness of the school created. Once the list was completed, we began to perceive ironic circumstances. The students' freedom of movement throughout the school, the same factor that gave the school its vitality and student centeredness, was a breeding ground for a wide variety of problems. It seemed that unrestricted movement of students allowed, and in some instances encouraged, students to aimlessly float, to make disturbances that interfered with ongoing classes, and to cause other related problems. Each teacher handled the disturbances differently; some ignored them, others were strict, some referred violators to the principal, others punished students themselves. This inconsistency was the largest contributor to the teachers' differences in their perceptions of the school's goals. When asked, the teachers felt that between 10% and 40% percent of the students were chronic problems.

At this point, a combination of insights were synergistically created that enabled the staff to understand the nature of the problem in a new way. One by one, the following points were noted, leading up to the identification of a most creative problem-solving alternative.

1. *The school needed a consistent policy accepted by all teachers and the principal.*

2. *The policy needed to be flexible to allow various alternatives for different situations.*

3. *The majority of students should not be restricted because of a large minority.*

4. *The minority of students who created problems should not be ignored because of the needs of the majority.*

5. *Students should be encouraged to assume responsibility, and any policy should be based on improvement, not punishment.*

6. *The problems of Valley View were mostly related to traffic and movement outside the classroom. Discipline and instruction within the classroom posed no significant problem.*

Finally, an idea was conceived modeling a real-life system with which all students were familiar and one that met all the pre-conditions just listed. The plan shows how the three-dimensional approach can be used and adapted to a schoolwide situation. The staff developed a list of rules that encouraged free movement but

did not allow fighting, loud noises, or aimless wandering. Each student received a list of the rules and discussed them during class time. A test would be administered to any student who wanted it, and the students who passed were issued "movement permits." This step is the same as the testing step in the prevention dimension. These permits signified permission to have freedom of movement throughout the school. If a student was caught breaking a rule, he/she would have an infraction on his permit. Three infractions would revoke the permit until the offender met for three group meetings with other offenders, two teachers, and the school psychologist. The purpose of the meetings was to help the offenders learn how to cope with responsibilities, not to punish them. As long as a student had no permit, he had to travel with a partner, or "chauffeur," who did have a permit (this included bathroom privileges). After a two-month trial period, each student who had either less than three infractions or had attended three sessions was issued a permanent laminated license, complete with his/her picture. Three offenses against this license would result in loss of the license and would require attendance in three group sessions. Fighting was one rule violation that resulted in immediate loss of license. (This was also the only rule that was extended to include classroom behavior.)

This system has worked well, and the reasons for its success are applicable to Valley View or any school for that matter.

1. The teachers accepted the system, because it grew out of their needs and from their own efforts.

2. The principal genuinely supported the system.

3. Because all teachers accepted the system and followed the rules, they created a consistent atmosphere for the students, who always knew what was expected of them.

4. No one teacher was responsible for loss of the student's privilege. It took three infractions to cause a loss of license.

5. *The system was built upon the need to give students responsibility. Those students who could accept responsibility were given it. Those that could not received help, not punishment.*

6. *The students understood the system—because of the familiarity of the driver's license analogy—and accepted it.*

7. *The effects of misbehaving were immediate. The infraction was immediately listed on the permit.*

There were additional management problems that the teachers faced when the system first began. The younger students lost many permits, over and over again, most likely because they had difficulty understanding the system. There was a great increase in paperwork for all the teachers. Some students found loopholes and were able to beat the system (by accidentally losing a permit that recorded an infraction). But the staff handled these problems in stride and found ways to solve them.

The permit/license concept enhanced the enthusiasm of the entire school and the community at large because everyone could relate to the concept. More important, however, was the interaction between teachers and principal. First, the staff began to talk about their goals, beliefs, and philosophies in a positive and supportive atmosphere, which enabled them to focus on a cooperative school environment rather than 30 isolated microcosms. Second, they were able to discern the difference between a goal and the methods used to reach that goal. This was a most critical step in the development of solutions. In addition, they saw the need to help students learn to be responsible by giving them more responsibility. Those that needed help could now receive it, without resorting to a restrictive and closed school environment. Finally, they participated in the development of an ongoing communication system among themselves and with the principal.

What we can learn from the Valley View experience is that there are a number of factors that contribute to successful programs for schoolwide discipline. The same basic factors that make the three-dimensional approach successful in the classroom are important for schoolwide problems. It is not necessary to develop an elaborate plan such as movement licenses, although the concept can work in most schools regardless of grades or location. What is important is communication and consensus.

Sandra Hughes, principal at Pepper Tree Elementary School in Upland, California, offers insight into the process(es) that make for an effective program in "Discipline with Dignity." She writes:

I am the principal of an elementary school which opened its doors last September. Pepper Tree is a K–6 school with 730 students and a certified and classified staff of 60 people. Upland is located about 30 miles from Los Angeles.

As an entire school staff, we have been on an exciting and rejuvenating journey this past year, adopting the "Discipline with Dignity" philosophy as the basis of our schoolwide behavior plan. I'm writing to share our journey, our learnings, and our next steps as we implement an entirely different approach to student discipline and adult teaching.

In the spring, I hired the teaching staff. We met together for two days right after school was out to get to know one another and plan for summer committee work, since the new school had nothing but a name. One major area of concern was that of a schoolwide behavior plan. We had all come from schools that used the punishment model—adult-determined school rules, citations for infractions of rules, a lock-step system of giving out punishments regardless of student needs. At that time, the staff discussed what they liked about their previous systems and what they didn't like. There was almost a unanimous feeling that the old system was lacking in many ways. They didn't like citations, blanket punishments regardless of the situation, and the fact that the same students were unsuccessful all year by constantly "being in trouble." This created great frustration, and teachers tended to see the failure as the students', not the system's. In short, we knew that we wanted something else for our new school, but we didn't know what that "something else" should look like. We did generate a list of ideas of what was important to us and turned the list over to a summer School Climate Committee. The charge to the committee was to develop a schoolwide behavior plan, share it with the rest of the staff through the mail, and have an inservice prepared for September so that we could begin school with the plan in place.

The School Climate Committee was composed of 10 teachers (all interested teachers were welcome), three parents, the District psychologist assigned to our school, and me. We met weekly throughout the summer. The meetings during the first month were difficult. We knew what we didn't want, but we didn't know what we wanted. We were searching not only for a philosophical foundation, but also for a system vehicle that would embody our values and goals and provide the structural framework to function with ourselves and with students.

Five years ago, as a fledgling principal, I received a copy of Discipline with Dignity *in an ASCD mailing. I had "always meant to read it but never quite got around to it." During this frustrating time of feeling rudderless as a committee, I picked up the book and started reading it. There was the philosophy that we were grasping for. I finally understood why we hated where we had been and what the goals of our plan needed to be. Over the next few weeks, the committee read it in sections and discussed the ideas at length. Our vision of changing attitudes about behavior at our new school was beginning to take shape.*

The challenge for the remainder of the summer was to develop the structural framework for implementing the "Discipline with Dignity" philosophy. Slowly we established our values, which we called "Cornerstones to Success." We devised a plan for involving students in the development of school rules. The plan also included training adults and students alike to think in terms of logical consequences rather than non-related punishments. We worked on some support systems for working with difficult students in order to assist teachers as well as other staff members in being proactive with those students rather than resorting to reactive, angry responses. We then sent copies of the book and packets of our "work in progress" to all staff members not on the committee. In doing so, the staff would have an opportunity to build a solid foundation before being inserviced on the plan during our pre-school meetings.

During the pre-school inservice we presented the plan. We walked through each step from goals to principles to rules to enforcement/intervention procedures to evaluation. We practiced making up an array of logical consequences for a rule infraction to apply the concept of "fair but not equal." We role-played talking to students about a rule infraction and saw that the interactions were quite different from our old "chew the kid out and set him/her straight" mode. For some of us, the dialogue was very uncomfortable, and we realized that we would have to learn to break some pretty entrenched behaviors in ourselves.

Once school started, each teacher worked with students to generate rules and consequences for each of our "Cornerstones to Success." For example, one of the cornerstones says, "Take care of personal and school property." Students considered, "How does that look in the classroom, on the playground, in the cafeteria?" We developed schoolwide committees incorporating teachers, students, and parents to finalize the rules for each cornerstone, synthesizing the thinking from all the classroom discussions.

Throughout the year, we have emphasized the rules as the way our school family needs to live in order to be safe and productive together. In dealing with students individually about rule infractions, we have applied logical consequences with this thinking: "What have you done that is not appropriate? Why is it not an appropriate action? How is it harmful? What can you do to fix it and make it right?" The emphasis has been on dialogue and drawing the answers from the students rather than lecturing with a pointed finger. We have incorporated into our classroom routines Stephen Glenn's class meetings. They have been the perfect vehicle for teaching students to see the specific good in each other and communicate it and solve their interpersonal problems in a dignifying, respectful, productive manner.

We have learned many things this year and feel that we've only scratched the surface of creating an environment that develops human beings in a caring, nurturing fashion. Here are some of my thoughts on the learnings:

1. *As adults in the school, we have become facilitators of student thinking and growth. We have become teachers and counselors in helping students to learn about their behavior. We are teaching behavioral skills and teaching students to be direct and upfront with each other rather than reactive and out of control. We are teaching students to express their feelings and respond to the needs of one another.*

2. *Because of the above, as an adult it is no longer necessary to control and "make children behave." That change in awareness takes a tremendous load from our shoulders and greatly reduces adult anger when children don't behave. My job is not to have them be perfectly behaved, but to work with them in an instructive way to help them understand the problem and fix it when they don't behave. We*

are allowing them to be children rather than expecting them to be robots.

3. This approach is very time-consuming, and sometimes it's difficult to give the time simply because it's not there.

4. Students show amazing ability to think critically when they are given the opportunity to problem-solve in a class meeting. We are lessening the "I don't know" response and the shrugging of the shoulders when asking students to talk about their behavior. One parent shared this response from her son when she asked him for an appropriate consequence to a problem he was having at home: "But, Mom, you know I hate to think!"

5. Adults and children alike are getting good at matching the consequence with a problem. Both groups are empowered in the process, and it's not all the adult's responsibility to right the wrong.

6. We've so ingrained children with non-connected punishment that it will take some time for them to fully realize their learnings. One sixth-grade student was caught cheating on a district test. His consequence was to meet with the District Director of Testing to talk about the incident and the resultant learnings. The discussion was a powerful one, but his statement to friends upon returning to class was, "I wasn't busted!"

7. In all of the workings of the plan, it is the process that's important, not the outcomes. Focusing on process gives adults resiliency and patience as they continue to teach human skills to children.

8. Kids are demonstrating a willingness and an ability to move out of themselves and be more accepting of others.

They are learning to put themselves in the shoes of others so that they see a problem from several points of view.

SITUATION

How can I make inroads with staff who just will not change their ways? I am a building administrator, and I often feel frustrated with some of my staff. Some keep just doing things the same way as always, and, with today's kids being what they are, the old ways aren't working. That leads to an endless parade of students sent by a few teachers to the office for correction. The attitude of some of these teachers is that it is not their job to be parent, caregiver, or mentor. They believe they are paid to teach and that is what they will do no matter how many or how few are interested in learning from them. Any thoughts on how I can deal with such staff?

ANALYSIS / SOLUTION

You are talking about mobilizing changed attitudes along with changed behavior. Just as such a process takes time with students, even in the best-case scenario in which the teacher wants to change, doing so is not easy and is best done gradually. People change slowly by trying something a little different in an atmosphere of support, and the experience of success sets the stage for taking the next small risk. As a principal, your job is to help each of your staff see how change can occur without requiring major changes in their current framework. Staff resist change when:

1. They do not know how to change.

2. They do not see how they will benefit from the change.

3. They see the change as needing to occur within the student(s).

4. They see others (parent or principal) as responsible for facilitating change.

In most instances, it is a combination of the above four factors that leads to resistance. Even when something is not working, people will not abandon the method until they have something else with which to replace it. Therefore, in order for a teacher to start sending fewer kids out of the room or the same kids out less often, they need to believe that they have other, effective ways of dealing with the problems that eventually make them refer the student. Simply telling them not to refer will not solve the problem. Just as some students need "lines" to use when they are stressed or verbally attacked by another, so too do some teachers need "lines" to say other than, "Out of here . . . . That's detention . . . . You can leave!" You must ensure that your staff has the skills needed to effectively deal with today's students. In my workshops, I often begin by asking veteran teachers with at least 10 years' experience the following questions:

(a) "How many of you think that, because you are more experienced, it is now easier than ever to deal with difficult student behavior?" Almost nobody raises a hand.

(b) "How many have found the challenge of dealing with difficult student behavior today to be about the same as always?" A few people raise their hands.

(c) "How many find that, even though you are more experienced, dealing with difficult student behavior is tougher now than ever before?" The vast majority raise their hands.

The reality is that today we are dealing with a different, more complex student. Students have changed, and we must change to effectively make contact with them. I see two distinct categories of ways to facilitate change. (1) There is change "from the inside out." Methods described in this book, such as students becoming better at planning, learning more effective ways of dealing with conflict, and becoming more responsible through getting better at making choices, are examples. (2) "Outside-in" change suggests that the behavior of important others can strongly influence one's choices and decisions. Research has found that when teachers make small changes in their behavior, there are vast differences in the attitudes and motivational patterns of their students. Such things as calling on students more often, offering increased clues and hints, expanding "wait" time, and being physically closer to students can yield many positive changes. People are more likely to change when they understand the process of change, when they are not asked to do too much too differently too soon, and when they have skills that they believe will be more effective with the contemporary student.

People embrace change when they see how they will personally benefit. Both children and adults need to try new things gradually and keep changes from within minimal to moderate. They must experience success in order to feel optimistic that change will lead to improvement. Those who resist change tend to be unhappy at what they do. They are unable to see how doing things differently will improve themselves or others. For a teacher to consider a different way, she must see how doing it differently will benefit the child as well as herself. I like to remind educators that kids who are discipline problems generally make them feel angry, frustrated, upset, annoyed. When this happens enough, the teacher loses patience, tolerance is reduced, and burn-out is in sight. There needs to be an acknowledgment that "misery" is probably what such teachers are feeling. It would be nice if those kids changed and did things as they should, but, if they do not, that misery is likely to continue if no changes are made in the educator's approach. While any change creates uncertainty and some apprehension, teachers need to view it in the context of, "What do I have to lose by trying it differently? If it doesn't work out, I haven't really lost anything. I can always go back to my old ways." You can encourage people's change processes by reminding them of this when dealing with issues of behavior and discipline. "Things now aren't going well, so even if I change and that doesn't work, I am no worse off than I was."

Finally, discipline today is everybody's business. Everybody who refuses to be part of the solution becomes part of the problem. As an administrator, your job is to inspire your staff to seek ways of making your school a better, more effective place than it is now. They must know that you are there for them, supportive of them, and that you have a sensible, doable vision. They must be *active* partners in seeking solutions to problems regarding discipline. When teachers and administrators work collaboratively, students benefit.

9

Concluding Thoughts

A FEW YEARS AGO, I was "remote-controlling" my way through the night when I unexpectedly came upon a Leo Buscaglia broadcast. I often find his words personally inspirational, so I listened to him describe the extraordinary stresses that contemporary mothers face. His wish was for there to be parks set aside only for mothers, where they could enter the gates and be greeted by a menu of personally rejuvenating experiences. Their energy sources could become refueled, and they could continue their work of meeting the needs of those who depend upon them. Buscaglia's talk applies to today's educator.

Working with children these days requires an endless supply of caring, concern, patience, enthusiasm, encouragement, sensitivity, and wisdom. There seems to be a never-ending parade of hurt, discouraged children who desperately need genuine affirmation of their worth. Many such children are afraid to risk trusting for fear of rejection. They may bond one day only to push away the next. They need at least one person in their lives whose message is:

"I refuse to reject you despite your best efforts at making yourself unattractive, unconcerned, and unmotivated. I will not agree to see you as a person of little value even though you believe this of yourself. I don't buy that. In this place, you can be successful, and I am tougher at insisting upon that than you are at insisting that you aren't worth the effort. I may get frustrated, angry, and even enraged with you at times. I will need to take occasional vacations from you, *but* I am not now nor am I ever going to give up on you."

This same attitude needs to be applied in working with groups of children and parents.

Take good emotional care of yourself. Be giving and loving to yourself so that you will have the strength it takes to really make an impact with kids. Most of all, be a "mensch" (someone who does the right thing because it is the right thing to do). Model and live respect and dignity for yourself and others.

Chris Boehm, a high school student at Webster High School in Webster, New York, wrote:

> *Teachers watch us, year after year. Students go in and come out. I suppose it becomes something of an assembly line. Students come in, you try to slap a nut or a bolt of knowledge into his/her brain, and then you move on. If teachers fall into this trap, though, they won't be the only ones who suffer . . . . An uncaring attitude spreads. If the teacher doesn't care, then neither do the students. Students can sense an uncaring teacher easily, and then act accordingly.*

For some students and their parents, sustaining a caring, dignified approach can be overwhelming. Gordon Dorway, an inner-city teacher, shows what is needed to reach many of today's students. After spending $150 on food for a barbecue at his house for his students and their families, of which 15 attended, he said, "What can I say? What can I do? You can't get angry. You can't get upset." Despite feeling discouraged, Dorway plans to start making home visits and might even give another barbecue.

An essential attitude for today's educator, especially when she is surrounded by overwhelming social circumstances that may make many with a caring heart feel hopeless, is offered by Viktor Frankl. This great philosopher, psychologist, and Holocaust survivor has said, "In a place where there are no human beings . . . strive to be human."

Bibliography

Armstrong, T. *In Their Own Way*. Los Angeles: Jeremy Tarcher, 1987.

Birdwhistell, R.L. *Introduction to Kinesics*. Louisville, KY: University of Louisville Press, 1952.

Brainard, B., and S. Behr. *Soup Should Be Seen, Not Heard! The Kids' Etiquette Book*. New York: Dell, 1990.

Brendtro, L.K., M. Brokenleg, and S. Van Bockern. *Reclaiming Youth at Risk*. Bloomington, IN: National Educational Service, 1990.

Camp, B.W., G.E. Blom, F. Herbert, and W.J. van Doorninck. "Think Aloud: A Program for Developing Self-Control in Young Aggressive Boys." *Journal of Abnormal Child Psychology* 5:7 (1977).

Curwin, R., and A. Mendler. *Am I in Trouble? Using Discipline to Teach Young Children Responsibility*. Santa Cruz, CA: Network Publications, 1990.

_____. *The Discipline Book: A Complete Guide to School and Classroom Management.* Reston, VA: Reston Publishing Co., 1980.

_____. *Discipline with Dignity.* Reston, VA: Association for Supervision and Curriculum Development, 1988.

Frankl, V. *Man's Search for Meaning.* New York: Pocket Books, 1963.

Freiberg, P. "Separate Classes for Black Males?" *The American Psychological Association Monitor* 22:5 (May 1991).

Gardner, H. *Frames of Mind.* New York: Basic Books, 1983.

Gentile, L., and M. McMillan. "Humor and the Reading Program." *Journal of Reading* 21:4 (1978).

Glasser, W. *Control Theory: A New Explanation of How We Control Our Lives.* New York: Harper & Row, 1984.

Glasser, W. *The Quality School.* New York: Harper & Row, 1990.

Kerman, S. "Teacher Expectations and Student Achievement." *The Kappan* 60:10 (June 1979).

Kohn, A. *The Brighter Side of Human Nature: Altruism and Empathy in Everyday Life.* New York: Basic Books, 1990.

Luks, A. "Helper's High." *Psychology Today* (October 1988).

Meichenbaum, D. *Cognitive Behavior Modification.* New York: Plenum Press, 1977.

Mendler, A. "From Where I Sit" (editorial on self-esteem). *Family Life Educator* 9:1 (Fall 1990).

_____. *Smiling at Yourself: Educating Young Children About Stress and Self-Esteem.* Santa Cruz, CA: Network Publications, 1990.

Mendler, A., and R. Curwin. *Taking Charge in the Classroom.* Reston, VA: Reston Publishing Co., 1983.

Molnar, A., and B. Lindquist. *Changing Problem Behavior in Schools*. San Francisco: Jossey-Bass, 1989.

Samenow, S.E. *Inside the Criminal Mind*. New York: Times Books, 1984.

Simner, M.L. "Newborn's Response to the Cry of Another Infant." *Developmental Psychology* 5 (1971).

Wlodkowski, R., and J. Jaynes. *Eager to Learn*. San Francisco: Jossey-Bass, 1990.

Zahn-Wexler, C., and M. Radke-Yarrow. "The Development of Altruism: Alternative Research Strategies." In *The Development of Prosocial Behavior in Young Children*, ed. Nancy Eisenberg-Berg. New York: Academic Press, 1982.

About *What Do I Do When . . . ?*
How to Achieve Discipline with Dignity in the Classroom and the National Educational Service

The mission of the National Educational Service is to help create environments in which **all** children and youth will succeed. *What Do I Do When . . . ? How to Achieve Discipline with Dignity in the Classroom* is just one of many resources and staff development opporutnities we provide that focus on building a **Community Circle of Caring**™. If you have any questions, comments, articles, manuscripts, or youth art you would like us to consider for publication, please contact us at the address below.

Staff Development Opportunities Include:

Discipline with Dignity
Managing Disruptive Behavior
Ensuring Safe Schools
Improving Schools through Quality Leadership
Integrating Technology Effectively
Creating Professional Learning Communities
Building Cultural Bridges
Reclaiming Youth At Risk
Working with Today's Families

National Educational Service
1252 Loesch Road
Bloomington, IN 47404
(812) 336-7700
(888) 763-9045 (toll free)
FAX (812) 336-7790
e-mail: nes@nesonline.com
www.nesonline.com

NEED MORE COPIES OR ADDITIONAL RESOURCES ON THIS TOPIC?

Need more copies of this book? Want your own copy? Need additional resources on this topic? If so, you can order additional materials by using this form or by calling us toll free at (888) 763-9045 or (812) 336-7700. Or you can order by FAX at (812) 336-7790.

Preview any resource for 30 days without obligation. If you are not completely satisfied, simply return it within 30 days of receiving it and owe nothing.

Title	Price*	Quantity	Total
What Do I Do When...? How to Achieve Discipline with Dignity	$ 21.95		
Discipline with Dignity (three-video set and Comprehensive Guide)	445.00		
As Tough As Necessary (four-video set and Facilitator Guide)	495.00		
How to Create Alternative, Magnet, and Charter Schools That Work	22.95		
Set Straight on Bullies (video and Facilitator's Guide)	139.00		
Anger Management for Youth: Stemming Aggression and Violence	22.95		
Rediscovering Hope: Our Greatest Teaching Strategy	19.95		
From Rage to Hope: Strategies for Reclaiming Black and Hispanic Students	19.95		
Reclaiming Youth At Risk: Our Hope for the Future	21.95		
Reconnecting Youth: A Peer Group Approach to Building Life Skills	139.00		
Safe Schools: A Handbook for Violence Prevention	25.00		
Dealing with Youth Violence: What Schools and Communities Need to Know	18.95		
Containing Crisis: A Guide for Managing School Emergencies	19.95		
Breaking the Cycle of Violence (two-video set and Leader's Guide)	325.00		
The Bullying Prevention Handbook	21.95		
Please add $3 handling and 5% of sales for regular domestic shipments within continental U.S.; or $5 handling and 7% of sales for special and/or non-domestic shipments.			

*Price subject to change without notice.   TOTAL _____

❏ Check enclosed   ❏ Please bill me (P.O. #_____)
❏ Money Order   ❏ VISA, MasterCard, Discover, or American Express

Credit Card No._____ Exp. Date_____
Cardholder Signature_____

Ship to:
Name_____ Title _____
Organization _____
Address_____
City_____ State_____ ZIP _____
Phone_____ FAX _____

National Educational Service
1252 Loesch Road
Bloomington, IN 47404
(812) 336-7700 • (888) 763-9045 (toll free)
FAX (812) 336-7790
e-mail: nes@nesonline.com • www.nesonline.com